HIKING WITH KIDS
NORTHERN CALIFORNIA

HELP US KEEP THIS GUIDE UP TO DATE

Every effort has been made by the authors and editors to make this guide as accurate and useful as possible. However, many things can change after a guide is published—trails are rerouted, regulations change, techniques evolve, facilities come under new management, etc.

We appreciate hearing from you concerning your experiences with this guide and how you feel it could be improved and kept up to date. While we may not be able to respond to all comments and suggestions, we'll take them to heart, and we'll also make certain to share them with the authors. Please send your comments and suggestions to editorial@globepequot.com.

Thanks for your input, and happy trails!

HIKING WITH KIDS
NORTHERN CALIFORNIA

42 GREAT HIKES FOR FAMILIES

Heather Balogh Rochfort
and William M. Rochfort Jr.

FALCONGUIDES

ESSEX, CONNECTICUT

For Liliana, always. Thank you for choosing us to be your parents.

And for my Anna—for initially instilling my love of wilderness in Northern California, and for then giving me a lifetime of love for the alpine. —WMR

FALCONGUIDES®

An imprint of Globe Pequot, the trade division of
The Rowman & Littlefield Publishing Group, Inc.
4501 Forbes Blvd., Ste. 200
Lanham, MD 20706
www.rowman.com

Falcon and FalconGuides are registered trademarks and Make Adventure Your Story is a trademark of The Rowman & Littlefield Publishing Group, Inc.

Distributed by NATIONAL BOOK NETWORK

Copyright © 2022 The Rowman & Littlefield Publishing Group, Inc.

Photos by William M Rochfort Jr.
Maps by The Rowman & Littlefield Publishing Group, Inc.

British Library Cataloguing in Publication Information available

Library of Congress Cataloging-in-Publication Data available

ISBN 978-1-4930-5832-7 (paper : alk. paper)
ISBN 978-1-4930-5833-4 (e-book)

∞™ The paper used in this publication meets the minimum requirements of American National Standard for Information Sciences—Permanence of Paper for Printed Library Materials, ANSI/ NISO Z39.48-1992.

The authors and The Rowman & Littlefield Publishing Group, Inc. assume no liability for accidents happening to, or injuries sustained by, readers who engage in the activities described in this book.

CONTENTS

INTRODUCTION 1

HOW TO USE THIS GUIDE 2

BEFORE YOU HIT THE TRAIL 4

MAP LEGEND 11

THE HIKES
Northern 12

1. Big Trees Loop 13
2. Boy Scout Tree Trail 19
3. Bumpass Hell Trail 25
4. Burney Falls Loop Trail 30
5. Cinder Cone Trail 35
6. Coastal Trail: Gold Bluffs Beach Section 40
7. College Cove Trail 44
8. Drury-Chaney Loop Trail 48
9. Elk Head Trail 53
10. Fern Canyon Loop Trail 57
11. Kings Creek Falls 62
12. Lady Bird Johnson Grove 67
13. Manzanita Lake Loop 72
14. Rim Trail 78
15. Stoney Creek Swim Area Trail 84
16. Stout Memorial Grove Trail 89
17. Subway Cave Lava Tube 95
18. Trinity Lakeshore Trail 100

Southern 107

19. 20 Lakes Basin: Steelhead Lake 108
20. Bartholomew Memorial Park Trail 113
21. Bodie Ghost Town Hike 118
22. Burst Rock 123
23. Ebbetts Peak 128
24. Leavitt Meadows to Lane Lake 134

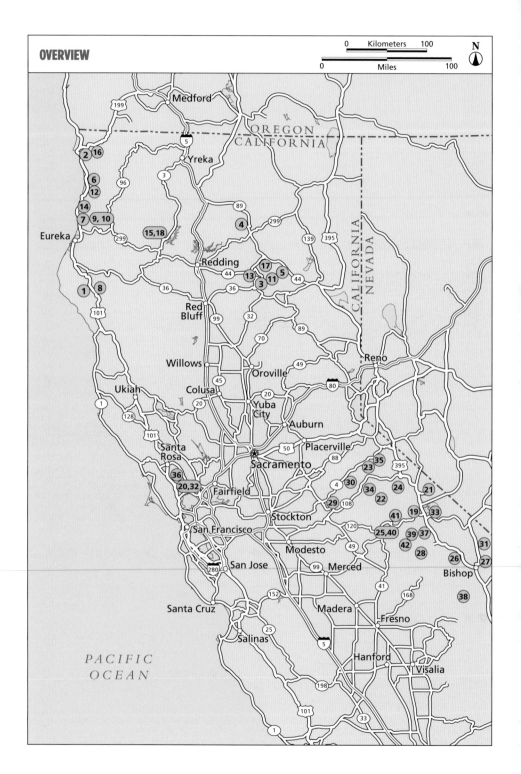

25. Lower Yosemite Falls Loop   139
26. McGhee Creek Canyon   145
27. Methuselah Trail   150
28. Minaret Vista Loop   156
29. Natural Bridges Trail   161
30. North Grove Trail   166
31. Patriarch Grove Trail   172
32. Sonoma Overlook Trail   177
33. South Tufa Trail   182
34. Trail of the Gargoyles: South Rim   187
35. Upper Kinney Lake via the Pacific Crest Trail   192
36. Wolf House Historic Trail   198
37. Yost Creek Trail: Fire Station to Ski Area   203

Advanced Hikes   208

38. Big Pine Lakes via North Fork of Big Pine Creek   209
39. Gem Lake via Rush Creek   216
40. Glacier Point Ski Hut   223
41. Glen Aulin   231
42. Thousand Island Lake Via Agnew Meadows   238

HIKE INDEX   246

ABOUT THE AUTHORS   247

Sunrise on Lassen Peak
from the top of the
Cinder Cone

INTRODUCTION

Only our family called it Beaver Rock, because of the way it looked from my Anna's back deck. It was one of many sea stacks in Marin, and it was particularly noteworthy for us because it was the largest and the farthest from my mom's mom's house (we don't say grandmother around these parts!).

Beaver Rock was a landmark for much of my early childhood, and I still remember the day when my parents told me that I was allowed to hike to it *and* climb it without supervision. I was several years short of getting a driver's license, but that permission—and the freedom that came with it—is when I first fell in love with Northern California.

Fast-forward a few years and I never lost the craving for that freedom. Even with a driver's license and, subsequently, a career with a paycheck, I wanted the feeling that's only found in nature. It feels like a cliché to write it, and it probably sounds like a cliché to read it. But, in today's state of perpetual connectivity, nature gifts us an opportunity for *presence* that is borderline impossible to replicate. Presence with yourself, presence with your family, presence with the living and breathing planet: Like many special experiences, words can only take you so close without being there yourself.

That's why books like this matter. My first guidebook was also a Falcon publication. After a couple years, their yellow spines filled a row of my bookshelf. And then a second row. I used the books to find my first backcountry experience in the Sierra. The north side of Thousand Island became my favorite patch of dirt on the planet, and I returned there over and over throughout my formative years to figure out who I was and who I wanted to be. It's the same reason our first multinight backpacking trip as a family was to the same destination. (Pro tip: Make sure you're prepared to cart out 10 pounds of diapers, but it's worth it.)

Personally, our family believes the value of guidebooks has grown exponentially in the digital age. The hikes you find in here aren't affected by algorithms, social media popularity, or their ability to contribute to clicks. They're a personal story about places we've found meaning, and we believe there are more than a few in here that aren't easily found on the first page of an internet search. We also endeavored to group these into collections of hikes you could do on a family weekend. If you're like us, there is significant effort in getting the family out the door for a hike . . . so if you're going to drive a few hours, you might as well have a couple of options in the area! This strategy also left out certain regions from this guide, because there's frankly too much of Northern California to put into a single book this size. So consider this a starter for inspiration. Then, do it the old-fashioned way and buy some local maps from a region you haven't yet explored.

—Will Rochfort

HOW TO USE THIS GUIDE

This guidebook is by no means a comprehensive resource, and it certainly cannot answer every single question you have about your planned hike. But then again, that is the beauty of hiking: the mystery you uncover around every bend in the trail.

We chose each trail for a specific reason. Perhaps a certain rock formation appealed to our daughter or maybe a glistening lake helped our family awake to a picture-perfect morning in the high alpine. Regardless, we know that all trails are different—and that all children handle them differently. For this reason, we have trails in this guide that run the full spectrum, ranging from beginner half-mile jaunts all the way up to 21-mile round-trip slogs that will challenge an experienced preteen. As parents to an avid hiker ourselves, we didn't want to assume that your kiddos could only handle the easy stuff. So, we made sure to include some challenging adventures so that you and the kids can keep returning for more.

The guide is divided into three sections: Northern, Southern, and Advanced Hikes. The hikes in the Northern section are all in the top half of Northern California, while those in the Southern section are in the lower half. Advanced hikes are significantly more challenging and are meant for older children (preteens and beyond) with hiking experience.

We've also tried to group a few hikes within an area. We know that families often travel for hiking vacations, and it feels more efficient to have a few options within a given area so that you don't drive 3 hours for a 20-minute hike.

Included with each route description are helpful pieces of information such as average hiking time, distance and elevation gain, trail surface, and potential child hazards. Driving directions are provided for the trailheads to each hike as well. Finally, a basic map is provided showing the trails and key points along the route. Each hiker is different and we understand that hiking times will vary widely from person to person, so we tried to estimate ballpark time frames as best as possible. Then again, your toddler may be faster than our own.

TYPES OF TRIPS

There are two categories of hikes you will see in this book:

Out-and-back: This means you will hike to a specific destination and then turn around to retrace your steps back to the trailhead.

Loop: This type of hike begins and ends at the same location with minimal retracing of your steps. If you look at the corresponding map, you will see that your route follows a loop-shaped pattern. In at least one instance, you will see the term *lollipop loop* used to describe a trail. This means you will hike for a distance, then complete a loop before retracing your steps back to the trailhead.

DIFFICULTY RATINGS

It is hard to standardize ratings of trail difficulty since it is largely subjective and depends on the individual, their fitness levels, and the required number of snack breaks. That said, I tried to standardize each hike as best as I could to help prepare for your adventures. In doing so, I used three categorizations:

Easy trails are suitable for any hiker, including the shortest of legs. The distances are typically less than 3 miles and there is less than 500 feet of elevation gain. Navigation is almost nonexistent, and you will never have to go off-trail.

Moderate trails are suitable for any hiker who has some experience outdoors and on the trail. These trails are anywhere from 3 to 5 miles in length and will have 500 to 1,000 feet of elevation gain. For children, these hikes may require some maneuvering or assistance from adults.

Strenuous trails are difficult and challenging hikes, meant for older children, those with ample on-trail experience, or for small children being carried in kid carriers by adults. These hikes are longer than 5 miles and will cover more than 1,000 feet in elevation gain.

TRAIL USE

The trails in this book are suitable for two types of adventures: hiking and backpacking, with the majority falling in the former category. The only difference between the two is that backpackers spend the night on the trail while hikers usually opt to return home. Backpackers prefer longer routes to justify camping outside, whereas day hikers frequently opt for less distance. You will see both categories of families on these trails—because yes, kids can and do go backpacking!—so be sure to smile and wave, even if your child is experiencing a full-scale meltdown. After all, you are all out there enjoying Mother Nature . . . and parents just get it, so no need to feel ashamed.

PERMITS AND FEES

Various land-management agencies utilize permits and fee structures, so you will see this vary from trail to trail. These fees and policies frequently change depending on the political climate and/or trail usage, so it is best to do research before leaving home. Call ahead to the local ranger station to be sure you don't show up to a trailhead empty-handed and permit-less when one is required.

And if you know permits are called for, yet you don't have one? Be kind; do not bandit the trail. Sure, it is possible that you will not get caught, but permits are in place for a reason, and it is not because rangers enjoy policing our nation's trails. Permits frequently regulate the quantity of visitors to help preserve our trails, so follow the rules. This makes the wilderness a safer place for everyone. One of our best purchases was the America the Beautiful annual pass, giving us included entrance to more than 2,000 federal recreation sites like national parks and national wildlife refuges, as well as covered day-use fees at Bureau of Land Management trails. The pass costs $80 per year, but it's more than worth it if you hike more than a few times.

BEFORE YOU HIT THE TRAIL

WEATHER AND SEASONS

Weather is the great equalizer of hiking. It does not matter how fit you are or how much you enjoy the trail; poor weather can ruin a trip if you are unprepared. Plan ahead by doing your research from home. Watch the weather weeks in advance, and as your trip draws closer, pay special attention to the weather patterns on your specific hike. Rainy weather is not always a reason to call off a trip, but communicate with others in your group. You may feel comfortable hiking through rain for 3 days, but your partners may not. Additionally, consider your altitude and topographical location if you see nasty weather in the forecast. Rainstorms above treeline frequently bring lightning and thunder, both meteorological occurrences that can be deadly. Some hikes are prone to lightning strikes, so double-check the weekend forecast before hitting the dirt.

Trail seasonality is highly subjective. For example, Glacier Point Ski Hut is going to look much different than Fern Canyon when January rolls around. Typically, summer and fall are the best seasons for hiking in the West.

If you plan on hiking a high-altitude trail, keep the cooler temperatures in mind. Agnew Meadows could be 85 and sunny, but it could be sleeting at Thousand Island Lake. Additionally, snow lasts much longer as you climb higher in the mountains, so plan on encountering a few snowfields if you hike above treeline in early spring.

If you do opt to head to higher elevations with your child, be sure to check with your pediatrician in advance. Depending on the kiddo's age and altitude experience, your doctor may have some specific suggestions for your family.

WILDFIRES

In recent years, wildfires have become a very serious problem in Northern California, with last summer remembered as one of the worst. Most of this book was researched and photographed prior to the Dixie and Caldor fires that blew through areas of Lassen National Park and Lake Tahoe. As a result, we've been cautious to ensure that the hikes in this guide will be open and available to families for hiking adventures. However, we can't predict Mother Nature (or restoration timelines), so we apologize if circumstances change between now and when you receive this book.

SAFETY, PREPARATION, AND GEAR

If there is only one piece of advice we can give you before your hike, it is this: Be Prepared! This has been the motto of every parent ever, and for good reason. If you plan accordingly and pack everything you need, there are very few instances where you will be caught in a bind . . . like that one time we forgot diapers.

THE TEN ESSENTIALS

First and foremost, always pack the Ten Essentials. The Ten Essentials were originally designed in the 1930s by The Mountaineers, a Seattle-based group of climbers and outdoor enthusiasts. In this original list, they included the ten items they felt any hiker would need to handle an emergency situation and safely spend a night or two outside. Since then, the original ten items have morphed into a systems-based list, but the ideology is the same. Theoretically, you will carry these systems with you on every hike, regardless of whether it is a multiday backpacking trip or a day-long hike. They are as follows:

1. *Navigation (map and compass)*: Be sure to always bring a topographic map with you on any trip, as well as a compass. Pro tip: While it's great to have these items in your backpack, it is even more important that you know how to use them! Store the map in a ziplocked bag or laminate it to ensure it doesn't get wet or destroyed. With modern technology, many hikers opt to carry GPS devices or even apps on their phone. While these are helpful and can be very useful, technology never replaces the tried-and-true map and compass. Gadgets break or quit or lose battery charge, but a map and compass will always work.

2. *Sun Protection (sunglasses and sunscreen)*: A sunburn can ruin any trip, so always take the necessary precautions. Wear a hat to protect your face as well as sunglasses to cover your eyes. Never forget sunscreen and lip balm with SPF, either.

3. *Insulation (extra clothing)*: Be sure to always have an extra layer or two in case of emergency. Perhaps you take an accidental digger into a stream while hopping across some slippery rocks? Or maybe your daughter poops her pants three times in 1 mile? You'll be psyched you brought extra clothing to keep everyone (and everything) in check.

4. *Illumination (headlamp or flashlight)*: It's rare for a hiker or backpacker to bring a flashlight, but headlamps can be very useful. It is always possible that you will conclude your hike in the dark. If this happens, a hands-free light will be absolutely critical. Also, cold weather can zap batteries, so make sure you bring an extra set with you on every trip.

5. *First-Aid Supplies*: Always, always bring medical supplies with you on every trip! And no, we're not simply talking about a box of adhesive bandages. Injuries happen on the trail, and if your partner sprains her ankle while you are trekking 7 miles from the trailhead, you will be very thankful for the splint. Additionally, be sure to bring the supplies that specifically apply to your babe. If you are hiking with a kiddo in diapers, diaper cream is always a good idea since kid carriers combine with heat to create wicked diaper rash. And, don't forget the wipes!

6. *Fire (matches or lighter)*: Not only will some sort of flame be helpful when it comes time to cook dinner, but these tools are useful if you need to start an emergency fire. These days, most hikers opt for lighters over matches. Whichever you prefer, bring a backup in case your Plan A doesn't work out. Additionally, consider bringing a fire starter with you on every trip. These can be made at home (dryer lint or cotton balls smeared with petroleum jelly are popular choices) and weigh next to nothing, so there is no reason not to carry a few.

7. *Repair Kit and Tools:* Your dog will pop your sleeping pad one time while winter camping and you will learn your lesson (could have happened to anyone . . .). Make sure you pack the basic repair tools on every trip so you can fix any gear emergencies that crop up.

8. *Nutrition (extra food):* Always pack extra food, regardless of how long you will be on the trail. If you are planning on a simple day hike, bring an extra day's worth of calories. If you know you'll be out there for a few nights, plan on more extra food. Regardless of what you choose, be sure the food keeps over time and doesn't require cooking. After all, your emergency situation may mean a stove isn't available either. And, don't forget child-specific snacks, especially if your kid is not old enough to pack their own. Now that our daughter is 3, we like fruit snacks because they work really well as perfectly timed bribery to encourage forward progress on the trail.

9. *Hydration (extra water):* Water is heavy (1 liter weighs roughly 2 pounds), but that doesn't mean you should skimp. Always pack extra to account for emergencies, and be sure to bring some type of filter or purification system so you can clean more if needed (and available). If your child is too young to manage water bottles or bladders on his own, don't forget a sippy cup.

10. *Emergency Shelter:* No one wants to sleep in a blizzard during an unplanned night out, but these things occasionally happen. And if it does, you want to ensure you are as safe and protected as possible. Bring an emergency shelter like a small bivy, tarp, or reflective blanket. Each option weighs only a few ounces but provides copious amounts of mental support.

BE BEAR SMART

Many of the hikes featured in this book run through bear country. After all, bears are everywhere! California does not have any grizzlies, so if you run into any bears they will be black bears. Regardless, it is a great idea to be prepared for the four-legged beast.

All About Black Bears

Black bears are the gentle giants of the bear world and can be found in all but ten of the lower forty-eight states. Here in California, they are especially predominant. While black bears may appear just as fierce and intimidating as a grizzly bear, it is better to think of them as playful cousins. They are much smaller than brown bears and are likely more concerned about finding your bag of food than finding you. Black bears are very smart and can climb trees, making them an annoying menace when it comes to food storage and caching. In fact, these bears are so intelligent that their problem-solving skills vetoed bear bags in favor of bear canisters in popular areas of California; they decoded the bear bag!

Food Storage in Bear Country

Keeping your food on lockdown is the best way to prevent bear interference with your trip. Many bear-heavy areas like Yosemite National Park require bear-resistant storage such as canisters or bear bags. If you opt for a bear bag, be sure you know and understand the guidelines for where to hang the bag and the appropriate distance from camp.

Likewise, if you use a bear canister, be sure you know the guidelines for where to stash your canister overnight.

Moreover, always be cognizant of your camp kitchen while backpacking in bear country. Never, ever cook inside your tent as the wafting smell of food may linger on your equipment and invite an unwelcome guest inside during the night. Instead, keep your sleeping location, your camp kitchen, and your food storage location as three distinctly separate areas, creating a triangle of sorts. While this isn't foolproof, it's an effective method to spread out the smell of human food and minimize the likelihood of a bear entering camp while you are sleeping.

If you are day hiking, you still need to be aware of food storage. Believe it or not, bears have been known to gain access to locked vehicles while parked at trailheads, all because they smelled a candy bar in the backseat. If you are hiking in bear country, be sure to transfer any and all food from your car to the food-storage lockers included in the parking lot.

LEAVE NO TRACE

Leave No Trace is a set of outdoor ethics designed to promote conservation and preservation in the backcountry, as well as minimize the human impact on our green spaces. The bedrock of this sustainability program is a list of seven guiding principles:

1. *Plan Ahead and Prepare*: Proper planning for any trip ensures you will leave as minimal an impact as possible. Know and understand high-usage times and avoid them. Research area-specific details so that you can better avoid causing further harm. For example, vegetation in high alpine zones takes 50 to 100 years to recover, so understanding this ahead of time may help you be more cautious in your actions.

2. *Travel and Camp on Durable Surfaces*: Good campsites are found, not made. Always try to pitch your tent on gravel, hard-packed dirt, rocks, or other sturdy surfaces as opposed to marsh or delicate grasses. Additionally, be sure to always camp at least 200 feet away from lakes and streams to minimize your influence on the aquatic plant life and wildlife.

3. *Dispose of Waste Properly*: Many people dislike speaking about bathroom behavior, but it's easily one of the most-discussed topics in the outdoors. We are all human, which means we certainly need to poop while on the trail. If this happens, no big deal, but follow the LNT-designed guidelines: dig a cathole of at least 6 to 8 inches deep and 200 feet away from water. Then, bury your poop in the hole, ensuring you properly cover it afterwards. And as for trash and litter? Pack it in, pack it out. And yes, this goes for diapers and wipes too.

4. *Minimize Campfire Impacts*: As synonymous as fires have become with camping, they are rarely a good idea since they cause lasting impacts to the environment and especially damage vegetation that takes years to recover. If you are camping in a dispersed area with a designated fire ring, keep it small and use only small sticks that can be snapped by hand. Be sure the fire is out completely before leaving it unattended.

5. *Leave What You Find*: Remember in kindergarten when we all learned to look but not touch? That same principle applies to the wilderness. If you happen upon ancient artifacts or historic structures, check 'em out, but let them be without altering or taking them. Likewise, don't create new structures, build trenches, or otherwise change the experience. Think about what the area looked like when you arrived, and then aim to leave it the same *or better* for the next person. This can be tricky when hiking with younger children who want to *touch everything*, but try your best to ensure your kiddo doesn't do any permanent damage.

6. *Respect Wildlife*: In recent years, the United States has seen an increase of human involvement with wildlife. Just because the mountain goats or deer come up to your campsite does not mean they are domestic; they are still wild animals. Never feed, follow, or approach these animals, and certainly try not to get too close. This is for both your safety and the animals' welfare.

7. *Be Considerate of Other Visitors*: We all hit the trail to gain a wilderness experience full of beauty and solitude. To that end, try your best to preserve that same experience for others. Don't blast your music while hiking or yell and shout late at night while camping close to others. Basically, mind your manners so everyone can equally enjoy their time outside.

Additionally, the 21st century has brought about a wave of new Leave No Trace discussions about the impact of social media. Thanks to the power of platforms like Instagram and Facebook, millions of users are geotagging specific locations while showcasing stunning scenery. In turn, hundreds and thousands of new visitors are heading to that specific location to see the real-life version of what they enjoyed in the photo. As a result, heavily photographed locations are becoming overrun and abused.

Leave No Trace recently released a brief list of suggested social media guidelines for the digital era. They included the following tips:

1. *Tag Thoughtfully*: Avoid geotagging specific locations and instead, tag the general area like "Rocky Mountain National Park." While this still encourages others to go outside, it protects the same locations from overuse.

2. *Be Mindful of What Your Images Portray*: So frequently, popular social media influencers showcase photos of picturesque scenes with a colorful tent pitched below a towering peak. But, there is one problem: That tent is pitched smack next to a body of water, and the account just subconsciously shared that with thousands of followers. Be aware of the images you share on your social media account to encourage your followers to conserve the wilderness just as you do.

3. *Give Back to Places You Love*: Get involved with volunteer projects to help give back to your favorite trails. These trails won't maintain themselves!

4. *Encourage and Inspire Leave No Trace in Your Social Media Posts*: Regardless of whether you have one hundred followers or 100,000, encourage them to take care of green spaces too.

HIKING TIPS AND SUGGESTIONS

There are two ways to look at this. First, we could go off the rails and detail all of the necessary gear and equipment that will make your adventure more comfortable and easier. We could talk about backpacks and hiking shoes, tents and sleeping bags. Or, we could remind you of the old adage: Hike your own hike. But what does that really mean?

We believe hiking newcomers frequently get caught up in all of the details and fancy-sounding words. If you walk into any outdoor goods store, you will be bombarded with words like *denier* and *ultralight* and *shank* and *outsole*. The stress is compounded if you're hoping to outfit your child—your most precious—as well. We don't want you to feel overwhelmed. Rather, we want you and your family to enjoy the fresh air and mental clarity that come from time well spent outdoors.

The spirit of this book lies within the variety of hikes features. Some of them are hard-core, meant for advanced hikers and older children, while others are mellow and brief, designed for first-time families with small children. Neither is right or wrong, and you have to decide which trail works best for you and your family. If you want to challenge yourself and your kids are ready for it, check out the hikes detailed in the Advanced Hikes section. There is no shortage of burning lungs and heavy backpacks on those trails. Or, if you are just beginning and/or want an easy day filled with encouragement, take a look at trails like the Subway Cave Lava Tube or Bodie Ghost Town Hike.

So again, we say: Hike your own hike and do whatever is best for your family on that particular day. That is up to you to decide.

PHOTOGRAPHY TIPS AND SUGGESTIONS

It does not matter whether you cart an elaborate camera with multiple lenses or a basic smartphone; you will certainly want to snap more than a few photos while on your hike. In doing so, you will accomplish the first requirement of great photography: getting out there. But once there, how can you ensure that you will shoot the best possible photos? Here are a few tips from Will Rochfort, coauthor of this book, experienced photographer, and the talent behind all the images found in this guide.

1. *Always have your camera accessible.* If it is a hassle to find it inside your backpack, you are less likely to take the time to shoot photos. Instead, find a system that works for you. If using a smartphone, store it in your pants pocket or in the waist belt pocket on your backpack. If you are using a larger camera, come up with a carrying method. For smaller point-and-shoots, a small camera case looped through the sternum strap on your backpack works very well. For larger DSLR cameras, a front-carry pack provides the same accessibility while acting as a counterbalance to your backpack.

2. *Focus on the light.* Dramatic subjects can look boring in flat light while mediocre subjects can appear downright dazzling with a beautiful evening glow. Focus your photography on the best capture of the light. Often this means shooting in the early morning or evening; often, the least flattering light is the overhead sunshine of midday.

3. *Carry a tripod.* Yes, this is extra weight, but your photos will thank you! It doesn't need to be fancy; a light, compact tripod will work. Find an option that you are willing to carry since stabilizing your camera may be crucial to many of your desired photos.

4. *Don't forget the extras.* If you shoot with a DSLR, remember to pack all of the extra equipment like memory cards, batteries, a cloth to clean your lenses, polarizers, and a charger if needed. There is nothing worse than setting up a shot of a stunning backcountry sunset only to realize that your "dead battery" light is flashing.

5. *Pixels are cheap.* It is a digital era, which means we don't pay to develop every single photo anymore. Snap as many photos as you want; you can sort through and delete the unwanted captures once you return home.

6. *Always grab the memory photos.* As a photographer, it is easy to get caught up in the "perfect" photos: a glorious sunrise, an action hiking shot, or a quick glimpse of an elk as she wanders through the wildflowers. But don't forget to take those often-cheesy photos with your group smiling at camp or posing by the trailhead sign. They won't feel as glamorous as your other photos, but these are the ones that help preserve your cherished memories. In our family, these classic standing-by-the-sign photos are the absolutely best to look at over time.

MAP LEGEND

〜80〜	Interstate Highway	≡	Bench
〜101〜	US Highway	⬦	Boat Launch
〜89〜	State Highway	≍	Bridge
〜4N12〜	County/Forest Road	■	Building/Point of Interest
——	Local Road	▲	Campground
== == ==	Unpaved Road	∩	Cave
⊢+⊢+⊢+⊣	Railroad	○	City/Town
– - – - –	State Border	—	Dam
··········	Featured Trail	•–•	Gate
- - - - -	Trail	▲	Mountain/Peak
∿	Small River/Creek	🅿	Parking
- ～ - ～	Intermittent Stream	≍	Pass
⬭	Body of Water	🎪	Picnic Area
	Marsh/Swamp	🏠	Ranger Station
⟃	Spring	🚻	Restrooms
≋	Waterfall	◄	Scenic View/Overlook
〰	Lava	🎿	Ski Area
▭	National Park/ Forest	①	Trailhead
▭	Wilderness	?	Visitor/Information Center
▭	State Park/Forest		

NORTHERN

Looking up toward the massive Burney Falls from the base

1 BIG TREES LOOP

Most visitors arrive at the Big Trees Day Use Area with the goal of spotting the Giant Tree, a massive redwood that was once considered the largest coastal redwood in the world. Bigger trees have since been discovered, but the Giant Tree is still worthy of a visit. Of course, that's not all you'll see on this hike since the mellow loop also takes you near the Big Tree, along with dozens of other magnificent leviathans.

Start: Big Tree Area trailhead
Distance: 0.7-mile loop
Hiking time: 30 minutes to 1 hour
Difficulty: Easy
Elevation gain: 10 feet
Trail surface: Dirt
Hours open: 24 hours
Best season: Any season
Water: At Albee Creek Campground
Toilets: At Albee Creek Campground
Nursing benches: Picnic tables at trailhead
Stroller-friendly: No
Potential child hazards: None

Other trail users: None
Dogs: Not allowed
Land status: California Department of Parks and Recreation
Nearest town: Redcrest
Fees and permits: Day-use fee
Maps: Humboldt Redwoods State Park brochure
Trail contact: Humboldt Redwoods State Park, 17119 Avenue of the Giants, Weott, CA 95571; (707) 946-2263; www.parks.ca.gov/?page_id=425
Gear suggestions: Sturdy shoes

FINDING THE TRAILHEAD

From Redding, take I-5 south for approximately 16 miles and take exit 662 for Bowman Road. Travel for 14 miles and then turn right onto CA 36 west and go 118 miles. Turn left to merge onto US 101 south and go 21.5 miles, and then take exit 663 and merge onto Bull Creek Flats Road. After a half-mile, the road turns into Lower Bull Creek Flats Road. Then again after a mile, it turns into Mattole Road. Parking is found at the Big Trees Day Use Area on the left side (south side) of the road. GPS: N40 21.71' / W123 59.52'

THE HIKE

It's no wonder that the Big Trees Trail is a popular choice among families. The gentle loop gains virtually no elevation, and it is a short enough distance that younger kids can manage it on their own. The real highlight, though, is the spectacular redwood groves that speckle the trailside throughout the entire route. The trees are massive, and not just in comparison to your kids. When combined with the dappled late–afternoon sunshine filtering through the skyscraping treetops, a visit to this peaceful paradise is a highlight for everyone in the family.

Begin your hike at the Big Trees Day Use Area and cross the seasonal footbridge that you'll encounter on the southwest side of the parking lot. Once you pass over the bridge, turn left and begin the loop in a clockwise direction.

For a brief moment, the trail skirts along the banks of Bull Creek, so the sounds of babbling water fill the thick silence shaking down from the gargantuan trees around you. While you're barely a couple hundred feet from the parking area, it feels as if you've

Looking up into the canopy at the start of the hike

Toppled trees like this one give a better sense of the redwoods' size.

GIANT TREE

RECOGNIZED BY THE AMERICAN FORESTRY
ASSOCIATION AS THE NATIONAL CHAMPION
COAST REDWOOD SEQUOIA SEMPERVIRENS
NOVEMBER, 1991

HEIGHT   363 FEET
CIRCUMFERENCE   53.2
AVERAGE CROWN SPREAD   52

At the base of the Giant Tree

Looking up toward the Giant Tree

walked into another universe where solitude and tranquility trump all else. While at the creek, take a look around to admire the expansive openness present at this point in the trail. With so little groundcover surrounding you, this is a great place to truly appreciate the sheer magnitude of these trees.

Continue past the sign for the Flatiron Tree and hike farther along the banks of the creek. Soon thereafter, you'll reach the Giant Tree. From here, you'll notice that many of the people turn around and return to their cars after having spotted the beast. We recommend that you complete the entire loop; there is so much more to see!

After the Giant Tree, the trail wraps into the forest, surrounded by lush greenery and soaring tree trunks. At 0.2 mile, you'll reach an intersection with the Bull Creek Flats Trail; turn right.

This stretch of trail highlights a multitude of midsize redwoods that aren't as large as the Giant Tree but still impressive all the same. A dense understory of the evergreen tanoak fills the lower horizon, providing a verdant landscape in an already-surreal environment.

As you continue hiking, the alluvial flat will open up, and as it does, you'll notice that the redwoods get bigger and the tanoak fades away. Just before you reach the next intersection, take a moment to observe: The tanoak is virtually gone now and in its place lives a beautiful grove of exclusively redwoods.

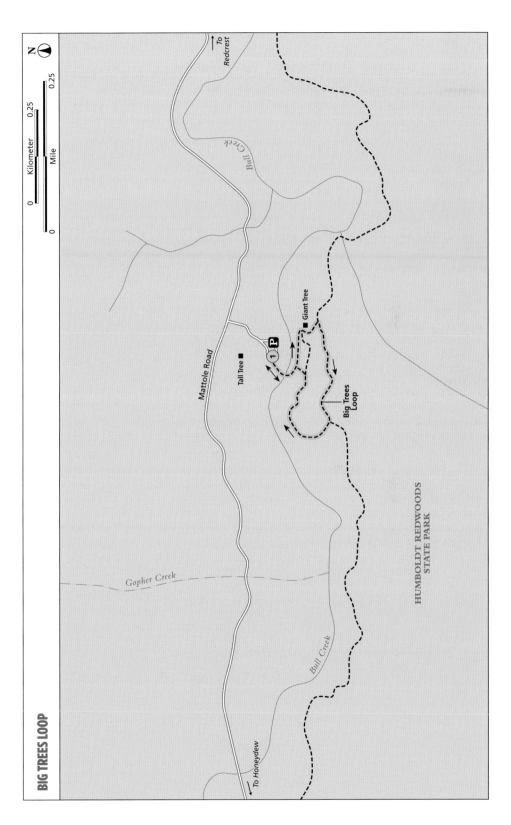

BIG TREES LOOP

FUN FACTOR: THE FOUNDERS TREE

Just down the road from the Big Trees Loop sits the Founders Tree, yet another magnificent tree that once held the title of being the biggest in the world. At 1,400 years old and 325 feet tall, the Founders Tree was known as the granddaddy from 1931 to 1957 when the Rockefeller Tree was discovered. But, there is a little controversy surrounding its height—or whether it was actually ever the tallest tree in the world. In 1964, scientists with the National Geographic Society measured the tree at 352.6 feet. Then, in 1968 a Humboldt State University professor measured Founders at 346.3 feet. Both of these measurements were noticeably shorter than the original 1931 height of 364 feet. While some believe the tree lost 18 feet during a violent storm, others believe the 1931 height was simply inaccurate and that Founders was never the tallest tree in the world. We'll never know!

You'll reach the trail split at 0.4 mile; stay right yet again. The trail to the left is the Bull Creek Flats Trail continuing through additional midsize redwoods. Instead, meander the last quarter-mile of this loop, enjoying a stretch of large redwoods that open into a glade filled with a high quantity of downed trees. The Flatiron Tree is one of them, but there are quite a few others to look at.

Close the loop trail by crossing back over the bridge and returning to the parking lot. For a fun mini-adventure after the hike, walk a few hundred yards to your left in the parking lot and look for a small trail. A few yards into the woods, you'll see the sign for the Tall Tree.

Also known as the Rockefeller Tree, the Tall Tree was the world's tallest known tree in 1957. Other trees subsequently stole its title, but it's still nice to visit. Plus, fewer hikers wander in this direction because it's not quite as impressive as the Giant Tree. Still, it's a nice way to end the day!

MILES AND DIRECTIONS

0.0 Start at the parking lot in the Big Trees Day Use Area. Begin in the southwest corner just before the wooden footbridge.

0.1 Stay left to begin the loop in a clockwise direction.

0.2 Reach the trail junction with Bull Creek Flats Trail. Turn right.

0.4 Arrive at a second trail junction with Bull Creek Flats Trail heading left. Stay right to continue onto Big Trees Trail.

0.6 Reach the end of your hike as you near the cars. Turn left.

0.7 Arrive back at the parking lot.

2 BOY SCOUT TREE TRAIL

Gargantuan redwoods line this ethereal trail tucked away off How-land Hill Road in Jedediah Smith Redwoods State Park. The drive to the trailhead itself is an adventure, but the true highlight is the magnificent old-growth redwood forests you'll hike through. While it is busy, you'll still feel utterly removed from the civilized world since you can't hear any traffic or noise beyond the forest. For us, that makes Boy Scout Tree Trail worth a visit on its own.

Start: Boy Scout Tree trailhead
Distance: 5.3-mile out-and-back
Hiking time: About 4 hours
Difficulty: Moderate
Elevation gain: 750 feet
Trail surface: Dirt
Hours open: Sunrise to sunset
Best season: Any season
Water: At the campground visitor center
Toilets: At the campground visitor center
Nursing benches: At Jedediah Smith Campground Picnic Area
Stroller-friendly: No
Potential child hazards: Poison oak along the trail edges and abundant amount of ticks

Other trail users: None
Dogs: Not allowed
Land status: California Department of Parks and Recreation
Nearest town: Crescent City
Fees and permits: Fee
Maps: Jedediah Smith Redwoods State Park brochure
Trail contact: Jedediah Smith Redwoods State Park, 1111 Second St., Crescent City, CA 95531; (707) 464-6101; https://www.parks.ca.gov/?page_id=413
Gear suggestions: Sturdy shoes and gaiters

FINDING THE TRAILHEAD

From Eureka, take US 101 north for approximately 79 miles. Turn right onto Humboldt Road and follow it for 1.5 miles. Turn right onto Howland Hill Road for approximately 3 miles. Parking is limited to small pullouts along the road with room for only a few vehicles. GPS: N41 46.13' / W124 6.62'

THE HIKE

We aren't joking when we say the drive to the trailhead is a worthy adventure. Your family vehicle will bump and jolt for over 2 miles down Howland Hill Road, moving deeper and deeper into the magical old-growth forests of Jedediah Smith. By the time you've arrived at the actual trailhead, you're likely to feel transported into another world.

While Boy Scout Tree Trail is a good hike at any point during the year, it's noticeably dazzling on sunny days when the beams of light filter through the canopy of trees up high. On stormy and cloudy days, the darkness can feel oppressive, so we recommend visiting when there is a bit of sun in the sky.

Out of the gates, the Boy Scout Tree Trail hits its stride. The largest trees of the hike live near the beginning, so you're immediately enveloped in a verdant and lush for-est filled with neon lichen and a plush undergrowth of ferns. It's easy to feel like you

Exploring the length of one of the downed redwoods

Careful when doing this; there are stories of people falling over backward as they look up.

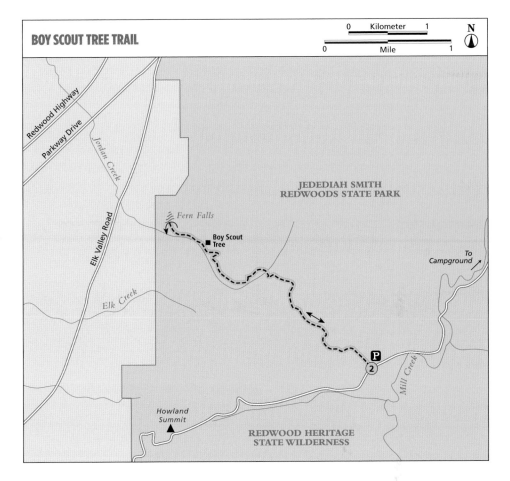

0   Kilometer   1

0   Mile   1

N

JEDEDIAH SMITH
REDWOODS STATE PARK

Fern Falls

Boy Scout
Tree

To
Campground

P
2

Redwood Highway

Parkway Drive

Jordan Creek

Elk Valley Road

Elk Creek

Mill Creek

Howland
Summit

REDWOOD HERITAGE
STATE WILDERNESS

shouldn't continue and instead, just sit quietly with these arboreal leviathans. Honestly, we wouldn't blame you—but we promise that the rest of the trail is pretty good too!

Unlike other trails in the region, there is a small amount of elevation gain on the Boy Scout Tree Trail, and you'll notice the climbing early in your adventure. You'll ascend nearly 200 feet in the first mile and, after a quick descent, climb up a couple hundred more. It feels gentle and it's very doable for kids of all ages.

After crossing a small stream and beginning the ascent, the forest opens up and allows more light inside. There isn't much soil to be seen; your entire surroundings are comprised of a dense fern understory with redwoods popping up sporadically. But the gradual openness allows hikers to better appreciate the sheer magnitude of these giant trees.

Eventually, you'll reach the ridgeline and the terrain will flatten out. Here, the trees also spread out and become fewer and farther between.

Descend back down from the ridge, now heading downhill until your turnaround point. You'll pass through forests of varying redwood densities, eventually crossing the itty-bitty Jordan Creek. Once you pass by the water, you'll soon enter a beautiful section of trail where a few lone redwoods fill the horizon. There aren't as many here as in other portions of the hike, but they are mighty. Since the trees are so sparse, it's easy to crank your head back and appreciate their grandeur unencumbered by a thick surrounding forest.

Balancing along the trail aside a girthy redwood

FUN FACTOR: PLAY AT THE PARK

As the nearest town, Crescent City is only a 20-minute drive from the Boy Scout Tree Trailhead. Once you're done hiking and the kiddos are begging for "fun time," we'd recommend heading downtown toward one of the coolest playgrounds we've visited. Tucked away at Beach Front Park and sandwiched between Front Street and the Crescent Harbor, the playground resembles a gigantic wooden fort, complete with slides, swings, and boardwalks. The ocean views are nice for the parents. And, bonus: You're right across the street from SeaQuake Brewing.

Continue hiking downhill to the bottom of the valley floor. Near the end, the redwoods gradually disappear; they naturally do not grow in this area. Just past 2 miles, you'll see a short, unmarked spur trailhead over to the right. This leg goes to the Boy Scout Tree, a huge double-tree that resembles a peace sign made with your fingers.

After the Boy Scout Tree, you're near the turnaround point at Fern Falls. While the name sounds spectacular, it's but a mere tiny cascade on the perimeter of the redwood forest. Once you arrive at the flowing water, turn around and retrace your steps back to the car.

MILES AND DIRECTIONS

0.0   Find the trailhead on the northwest side of Howland Hill Road.

1.1   Reach the top of your climb.

1.4   Cross the first stream at the base of your descent.

2.2   Trail junction; small spur trail to the right heads to the Boy Scout Tree.

2.65 You've reached Fern Falls. Turn around and retrace your steps back to the beginning.

3 BUMPASS HELL TRAIL

Come for the views, stay for the technicolor hot springs, and laugh alongside your kids giggling over the name "Bumpass Hell." To be sure, children love this hike for the almost-but-not-quite duo of foul words, but the bubbling mud pots, hissing steam vents, and egg odor are enough to bring families back time and time again.

Start: Bumpass trailhead (7 miles from the park's Southwest Entrance)
Distance: 3.0-mile out-and-back
Hiking time: About 2 hours
Difficulty: Easy
Elevation gain: 423 feet (most of which is getting back out of the basin)
Trail surface: Dirt, rock, and boardwalk
Hours open: Open daily, 24 hours a day, but the road to the trailhead is closed approximately from Nov until June depending on snow
Best season: Summer to early autumn
Water: Fill up at any of the visitor centers
Toilets: At the trailhead
Nursing benches: No
Stroller-friendly: No

Potential child hazards: Some steep ledges, very hot geothermal pools, and acidic mud and water around the geothermal pools
Other trail users: None
Dogs: Not allowed
Land status: National Park Service
Nearest town: Mineral
Fees and permits: Fee to enter the park, or purchase America the Beautiful annual pass
Maps: Lassen Volcanic National Park map
Trail contact: Lassen Volcanic National Park, PO Box 100, Mineral, CA 96063; (530) 595-4480; www .nps.gov/lavo
Gear suggestions: Sun protection and plenty of water due to limited amounts of shade along the trail

FINDING THE TRAILHEAD

From Redding, take CA 44 east for approximately 47 miles. Turn right to head south on CA 89 toward the park entrance. After 23 miles, the trailhead parking will be on your left. Parking is limited and usually fills up by midmorning especially on the weekends. GPS: N40 27.48' / W121 30.06'

THE HIKE

Here's a tip: You could start by telling your kids, "Hey, this is the largest hydrothermal area in the park!" But, we'd expect you to receive a dramatic series of eye rolls. Instead, start with this headliner: "Want to see the boiling mud pot that caused this guy to lose his leg?"

You can thank us later.

In all seriousness, Bumpass Hell is the best locale to witness geology in action inside Lassen National Park. The 16-acre area boasts churning springs, sizzling steamy vents, and water so acidic that it rivals the stuff inside our stomachs. In fact, the hike's name comes from the unfortunate explorer who discovered it—and lost a limb in the process.

In 1864, a cowboy and early explorer named Kendall Vanhook Bumpass was searching for lost cattle. While exploring the then-unknown region, his foot broke through the crunchy thin soil and dunked into the boiling mud pot hidden beneath the earth. The exceedingly hot mud scalded him, leading to an eventual amputation. Upon his return

Walking along the boardwalk that traverses the hydrothermal area

Talking science at the overlook at the far end of the trail

Pausing on the way back out to catch our breath and admire the pools

home, other townsfolk asked Bumpass where he'd been exploring and he responded with these immortal words: "Boys, I have been in hell."

And thus, Bumpass Hell found its name.

The geological ruckus below (and above) the surface stems back to a series of deep fissures in the earth. Bumpass would likely say that these cracks run so deep that they reach Hades, but in reality, the fissures tap into the volcanic heat that sits deep within the earth's core. Meanwhile, Mother Nature's natural moisture like rain or snow gradually seeps into these cracks and travels downward. When it runs into volcanically heated rock, a searing-hot steam erupts through the fissures. Bottom line: The temperature in Bumpass Hell pools can soar as high as 250 degrees Fahrenheit.

FUN FACTOR: DUNK IN AN ALPINE LAKE

Across the road from the Bumpass Hell trailhead is a glimmering body of water known as Lake Helen. The deep blue water is nestled up against the base of Lassen Peak and offers up one of the most majestic views in the park. As we all know, views don't always do it for kids—but polar plunges just might! At over 200 feet deep, Lake Helen often holds snow and ice until well into the summer (even July), so the water itself is made up of snowmelt. Of course, this makes it chilly. But, if you and your family time the visit just right and secure yourselves a bright and sunny day, we recommend taking the kiddos for your own version of a polar plunge. Don't forget a towel!

Views of volcanic peaks that oversee the beginning portions of the trail

It's sounds scary, but it's not—we promise. The Bumpass Hell hydrothermal area is much safer than it was during Bumpass's heyday, but it's still important to keep an eye on your children as they traverse the boardwalks and trails that run over the boiling pots. If you have a younger child or toddler who is unsteady on his feet, we recommend keeping him in a kid carrier to prevent any accidents.

The trail begins at the obvious and large parking area in Lassen National Park, next to the easily spotted sign that identifies the trailhead. The hike itself is a mellow stroll, and the first 0.2 mile remains relatively flat as the wide trail cuts into the side of the mountain. But as the trail wraps to the right and you approach 0.3 mile, it also begins climbing up to its high point of 8,400 feet.

At 0.5 mile (and between interpretive posts 10 and 11), your family will notice a small spur trail that jets off to the right. Not only is it worth a brief reprieve from the climb, but the tiny path heads to a beautiful overlook of Mount Conard, Diamond Peak, Brokeoff Mountain, Pilot Pinnacle, and Mount Diller. Once upon a time, these five peaks comprised a large ancient volcano named Mount Tehama that reached the massive height of 11,500 feet. Tehama has long since collapsed, but these are the remnants of that once-mighty volcano. In fact, Lassen Peak itself was formed from all of the hot lava that flowed from Tehama's explosion.

Continue hiking uphill until you reach the high point around 1.0 mile. You'll also begin to hear the strange sounds coming from Bumpass Hell, although you can't yet see it. But your nose will know it's coming! The sulfur scent wafts uphill as you descend into Bumpass Hell, and kids are typically grossed out by the "egg smell."

Descend a half-mile, following your nose toward the ubiquitous sulfur odor. At the base of the hill, the trail wraps left through a dense grove of trees. You'll emerge onto a wooden bridge that takes you over a small, milky-colored stream before depositing you onto the series of boardwalks. You've reached Bumpass Hell.

The boardwalk leads hikers up to and around the various mud pots and hissing steam vents, allowing your kids ample opportunity to admire the vivid yellows, oranges, and blues that stem from the minerals in the water. Even the stream looks like liquid cement as it flows through the region, thick and gray and acidic.

Follow the boardwalk around the hydrothermal sites, but don't forget to climb the small hill at the back of Bumpass Hell. It's a bit of a climb but the vantage point from the top is the best overall perspective of the entirety of Bumpass Hell, and it's not to be missed.

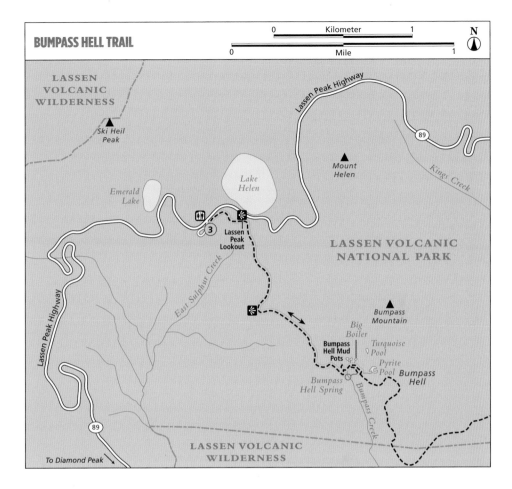

BUMPASS HELL TRAIL

Kilometer

Mile

N

LASSEN VOLCANIC WILDERNESS

Ski Heil Peak

Lassen Peak Highway

89

Mount Helen

Kings Creek

Lake Helen

Emerald Lake

East Sulphur Creek

Lassen Peak Lookout

LASSEN VOLCANIC NATIONAL PARK

Lassen Peak Highway

Bumpass Mountain

Big Boiler

Turquoise Pool

Bumpass Hell Mud Pots

Pyrite Pool

Bumpass Hell

Bumpass Hell Spring

Bumpass Creek

89

To Diamond Peak

LASSEN VOLCANIC WILDERNESS

(**Option:** If you have extra energy in the tank, your family can continue hiking an additional 1.5 miles to Cold Boiling Lake, a bubbling alpine lake.)

MILES AND DIRECTIONS

0.0 Begin at the Bumpass Hell Trailhead on the well-marked path that leaves from the east side of the parking lot by the entrance.

0.3 Snag your camera and snap a classic image of Lassen Peak reflected in the water of Lake Helen to your left.

0.5 Take a break from climbing to snap yet another photo of the overlook with views of Brokeoff and Diller Mountains in the distance to the right.

1.0 Begin your descent into Bumpass Hell.

1.2 Trail junction; stay right.

1.4 Cross the wooden bridge and find the boardwalk that wraps through Bumpass Hell.

1.5 Turn around and retrace your steps back to the parking area.

3.0 Arrive back at the trailhead.

4 BURNEY FALLS LOOP TRAIL

If you and the kids want to go chasing waterfalls, look no further than Burney Falls. The cascading, aqua-blue water will have you feeling like you've walked onto a tropical island—only a lot more accessible. Plus, nearby picnic areas and campgrounds make Burney one of the top choices for active kiddos on warm days.

Start: McArthur-Burney Falls Memorial State Park Visitor Center
Distance: 1.0-mile round-trip
Hiking time: About 1.5 hours
Difficulty: Easy
Elevation gain: 157 feet
Trail surface: Dirt and rock
Hours open: 8 a.m. to sunset
Best season: Late spring to early autumn
Water: At Burney Falls General Store
Toilets: At Burney Falls General Store
Nursing benches: No
Stroller-friendly: Yes, but only to the overlook

Potential child hazards: Slippery rocks near the waterfall
Other trail users: None
Dogs: Not allowed
Land status: California Department of Parks and Recreation
Nearest town: Burney
Fees and permits: Day-use fee
Maps: McArthur-Burney Falls Memorial State Park brochure
Trail contact: McArthur-Burney Falls Memorial State Park, 24898 CA 89, Burney, CA 96013; (530) 335-2777; www.parks.ca.gov/?page_id=455
Gear suggestions: Sturdy shoes

FINDING THE TRAILHEAD

From Redding, take CA 299 east for approximately 65 miles. At Four Corners, take a left onto CA 89 north and go 6 miles. Take a left onto Lake Road toward McArthur-Burney Falls Memorial State Park. The trailhead is just across the road from the visitor center. There is a large parking lot at the visitor center and more parking farther down Lake Road. GPS: N41 0.72' / W121 39.11'

THE HIKE

Our family has visited a few of the world's most incredible waterfalls like Niagara and Iguazu, so we felt a bit suspicious when we read that Theodore Roosevelt once referred to Burney Falls as the "Eighth Wonder of the World." Could this lesser-known waterfall tucked away to the northeast of Redding truly rival the giants?

In a word: yes.

The 129-foot Burney Falls is the centerpiece of McArthur-Burney Falls Memorial State Park, the second-oldest state park in California. The park itself sits within the Cascade Range and Modoc Plateau and boasts 910 acres of forest along with 5 miles of streamside and lake shoreline. While Burney isn't the tallest waterfall in the state or even the highest, it is frequently considered to be the most beautiful thanks to the myriad of whitecaps flowing over the side of the rock wall. This is a selling point for kids: You get to see *lots* of waterfalls! And, the crescendo lasts all summer long since Burney doesn't dry up like many other California waterfalls.

The secret: meltwater from the surrounding mountains. Lassen National Park sits 40 miles to the north, and its porous volcanic rock slowly releases the moisture that stems from rain and snow in the Pit River watershed. Often, the water directly flows into

The first view of the falls as you descend down to the pools

The well-maintained walkway makes comfortable walking for the start of the trail.

Burney Creek, the feeding stream of the waterfall. In low-water years, Burney Creek sinks into its bed and virtually disappears. But, it reappears as water seeping out from the underground springs and convening in a mystical and mist-filled basin that pools around the base of the waterfall.

It is possible to skip the trek and see the natural wonder from the parking lot, but the counterclockwise hike will take you a lot closer. And, we promise: It's worth the effort to witness more than 100 gallons of water per day thundering over the edge.

Begin the hike in the parking lot just a few steps away from the well-established overlook. For those unwilling to descend any farther, this view is darn good and a great spot to grab a quick overall scenery photo as the looming trees create the perfect picture frame for the falls.

From there, continue downhill on the path as it meanders through three long switchbacks that descend nearly 160 feet before depositing you at the base of the falls. Metal rails line the path so small children are relatively safe. And, there is a bench halfway down the switchbacks if you or the kids need to take a quick rest.

If you're short on time, you may opt to cut the hike short once you've reached the base of the falls at 0.1 mile. Regardless of whether you turn around or continue on the entire loop, this viewpoint is unparalleled. The pool is lined with a collection of large boulders that many hikers use as seats to admire the view. It's often shady down there and the billowing mist is like a built-in air-conditioner on hot days. During our most recent visit on a record-hot July afternoon, we observed a whopping 15-degree difference between the top and the bottom of the falls!

Once you've had your fill, continue hiking north alongside Burney Creek and away from the crowds gathering at the pool. When you reach 0.3 mile, you'll see the Rainbow Bridge that climbs over the creek. This means you've reached the bottom of the valley. Cross the bridge and follow the path as it turns south and climbs back up toward Burney Falls.

It's a gradual ascent with most of the climbing behind you by mile 0.6, but little legs may notice the effort. Since this portion of the trail hides the waterfalls—you can hear them but you can't see them!—kids often hit their low-energy point around here. Use the hidden overlook at 0.6 mile to encourage them to continue. Not only does the word *hidden* conjure up excitement, but the view itself is nice to see.

Climb for another tenth of a mile, enjoying views of the falls before arriving at a trail junction with the Pacific Crest Trail (PCT). If you head right, your family will venture onto the PCT itself. Stay left and once again cross the bridge that takes you back to the opposite side of Burney Creek and the road. The trail veers left and follows the road for 0.1 mile before returning you back to the trailhead.

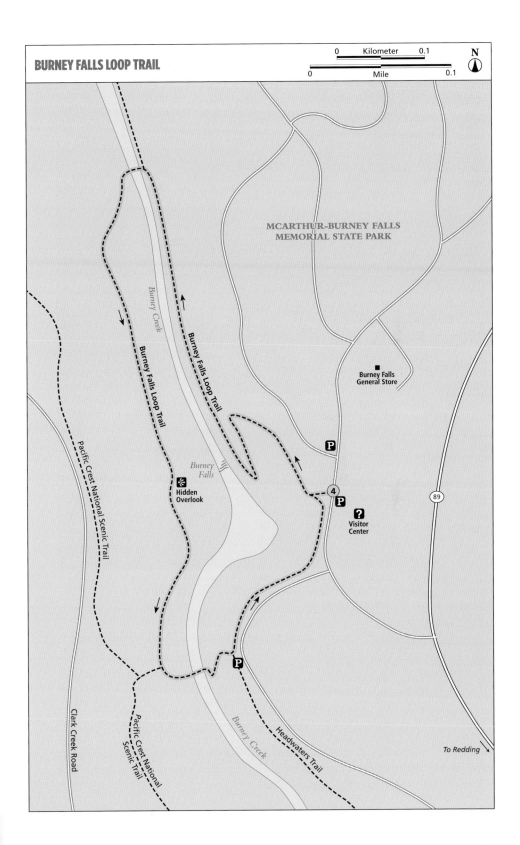

BURNEY FALLS LOOP TRAIL

0   Kilometer   0.1

0   Mile   0.1

N

MCARTHUR-BURNEY FALLS
MEMORIAL STATE PARK

Burney Creek

Burney Falls Loop Trail

Burney Falls Loop Trail

Burney Falls Loop Trail

Pacific Crest National Scenic Trail

Burney Falls
General Store

P

89

4

P

Visitor
Center

Burney
Falls

Hidden
Overlook

Clark Creek Road

Pacific Crest National Scenic Trail

P

Burney Creek

Headwaters Trail

To Redding

Hoofing it back out to the canyon rim

MILES AND DIRECTIONS

0.0 Begin the hike on the paved path at the overlook to the west of the main parking lot.

0.1 You've reached the bottom of the waterfalls; this is a good spot to sit and relax in the shade while admiring the scenery. Once you're done, continue hiking north alongside Burney Creek.

0.3 Turn left; cross the creek on Rainbow Bridge.

0.6 Find the hidden overlook on the left side to snag a special view of the waterfall.

0.7 Trail junction; stay left. The trail to the right is the Pacific Crest Trail.

0.8 Trail junction; stay left.

1.0 You've returned to the trailhead.

5 CINDER CONE TRAIL

This is one of our favorite views in Lassen National Park because the un-treed Cinder Cone summit gives incredible 360-degree views, and the remote trailhead typically means smaller crowds than in other parts of the park. The catch: This is perhaps the most grueling 4-mile hike in the book, as the steep incline around the Cinder Cone is doubly challenging due to the sandy floor that constantly shifts under your feet.

Start: Cinder Cone trailhead
Distance: 4.0-mile lollipop loop
Hiking time: About 3 hours
Difficulty: Moderate to strenuous
Elevation gain: 1,043 feet
Trail surface: Dirt and gravel
Hours open: Open daily, 24 hours a day, but the road to the trailhead is closed approximately from Nov until June depending on snow
Best season: Late spring to early autumn
Water: At Butte Lake Campground
Toilets: At the trailhead
Nursing benches: No
Stroller-friendly: No

Potential child hazards: Loose gravel around the Cinder Cone
Other trail users: None
Dogs: Not allowed
Land status: National Park Service
Nearest town: Old Station
Fees and permits: Fee to enter the park, or purchase America the Beautiful annual pass
Maps: Lassen Volcanic National Park map
Trail contact: Lassen Volcanic National Park, PO Box 100, Mineral, CA 96063; (530) 595-4480; www.nps.gov/lavo
Gear suggestions: Trekking poles and sturdy shoes

FINDING THE TRAILHEAD

From Redding, take CA 44 east for approximately 60 miles. Turn right to stay on Route 44 east toward signs for Susanville/Reno. If you see the Subway Cave Lava Tube on your right, you've missed the right to stay on CA 44. After 11 miles, turn right onto Butte Lake Road / FR 32N21. Follow the road until it ends at Butte Lake Campground after approximately 7 miles. Parking is just after the Butte Lake Ranger Station. GPS: N40 33.89' / W121 18.13'

THE HIKE

We highly recommend an early start in the summer, as the exposed terrain can get extremely hot. Once you're on the top, it's worth it; plus your kids can say they hiked to the top of a volcano! If you have the gumption to carry the extra weight, pack a picnic to enjoy on the edge of the crater; it will be one of your most memorable backcountry dining experiences.

The trail begins by the signed Butte Lake boat ramp, and it heads mostly southwest with only moderate elevation gain to start. The scenery is consistent with the lodgepole and Jeffrey pine forest you find in this part of the park, and the shade makes for a very pleasant amble through the woods. The start of the trail at Butte Lake overlays with the Nobles Emigrant Trail, a trail established in 1851 while William Noble searched for gold in the area. It was considered a shortcut to the Sacramento Valley and favored by travelers

One of the early views of the Cinder Cone, with the clear trail that wraps around

Looking down on the Painted Dunes

Peering into the base of the cone—it's a longer walk than it looks!

for its relatively consistent water sources along the way. As you walk along the sandy trail, picture what it was like trying to force a wagon through this terrain, and use this moment to remind your progeny that it is indeed possible to survive in the wilderness without Wi-Fi.

After about half a mile you'll pass the turn for Prospect Peak, which is a nice bonus hike if you find yourself with a layover day. The trail to Prospect Peak is also more heavily shaded, and it can provide nice cover if you find yourself here on an unexpectedly hot summer day.

FUN FACTOR: VISIT THE NATURAL RAINBOW

The Painted Dunes' shades of reds, yellows, and grays meld with each other across acres and acres of rolling black pumice dunes. If you can get here early or late in the day, it's almost impossible to take a bad photo. (Pro tip: Bring a telephoto if you want to compress the landscape from the high angle up on the Cinder Cone.) Like most things in the area, you can thank the region's volcanic activity for the watercolor-like palette. Ash fell on the lava flows when they were still hot, and as the ash oxidized, it changed to the hues you see here.

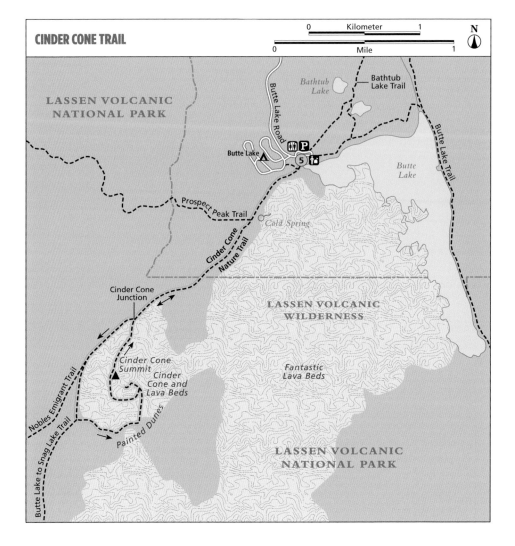

0   Kilometer   1

0   Mile   1

N

LASSEN VOLCANIC
NATIONAL PARK

Bathtub
Lake

Bathtub
Lake Trail

Butte Lake Road

Butte Lake Trail

Butte Lake

5

Butte
Lake

Prospect Peak Trail

Cold Spring

Cinder Cone
Nature Trail

Cinder Cone
Junction

LASSEN VOLCANIC
WILDERNESS

Nobles Emigrant Trail

Cinder Cone
Summit

Cinder
Cone and
Lava Beds

Fantastic
Lava Beds

Butte Lake to Snag Lake Trail

Painted Dunes

LASSEN VOLCANIC
NATIONAL PARK

Shortly after you'll walk by the sign for the Fantastic Lava Beds (definitely sounds like they were named by a group trying to drum up tourism interest), which are massive piles of basalt on the south side of the trail. Continue in a southwesterly direction and at about 1.5 miles you'll come to the base of the Cinder Cone, which accounts for 700 feet of the trail's 900 feet of elevation gain.

Gird your loins; hiking up the soft, loose scoria—commonly known as volcanic rock—is like hiking up a massive sand dune, and depending on the amount of weight in your kid carrier, your quads may be screaming before you even get halfway. Thankfully the views get better with every step, and you can pause as often as you like to gaze across the valley toward the 10,456-foot Lassen Peak.

Once you attain the crater rim, you will quickly forget the lung-busting grind to get to the top. In addition to the aforementioned Prospect Peak and Lassen Peak, you'll have views of Butte Lake, Snag Lake, the Red Cinder Cone, Chaos Crags, and Fairfield Peak.

If you follow the crater rim trail to the opposite side, you'll also look down upon the Painted Dunes.

Continue wandering the circumference of the crater, and if you don't mind a little extra elevation gain, you can follow a trail down to the base. The views don't improve significantly from the inside, but you will get a new appreciation for the sense of scale, and standing at the base of a volcanic crater is definitely an impressive box to check on the family list.

Once you've had your fill, simply return the way you came and enjoy the simplicity of walking *downhill* on piles of volcanic rock.

(**Side note:** If you're wondering if it's worth hiking to the base of the Cinder Cone without going to the top, we would say probably not. Given the commitment to get to this end of the park, we'd recommend saving the driving time and sticking to other portions of the park.)

MILES AND DIRECTIONS

0.0   Begin the hike on the trail that leaves from the south side of the parking lot.

0.4   Trail junction; stay left.

1.3   Trail junction; stay right. The trail to the left is a direct route up the cone but it's very steep.

1.4   Begin looping around the back of the Cinder Cone.

2.3   Start the steep climb up the back of the cone.

2.5   Be sure to look out and catch a glimpse of the Painted Dunes; it's a beautiful view!

2.7   You've reached the top of the cone. When you're done admiring the view, find the steeper trail running down the north side of the cone and descend there. Follow your steps back to the car.

4.0   Arrive back at the car.

6 COASTAL TRAIL: GOLD BLUFFS BEACH SECTION

The term *prairie* may invoke thoughts of homesteads and little houses in the central United States, yet this hike takes you through one of the California coastal variety. This short jaunt could easily turn into an all-day affair like it did for us; it's a long, beautiful walk on a beach with endless views of the Pacific Ocean. We spent as much time playing in the dunes, making sand castles, and chasing the waves as we did actual hiking, and we'd do it that way every time if given the choice. As an extra bonus you're likely to spot one of the resident herds of Roosevelt elk on your walk; this particular subspecies is the largest of the six in North America.

Start: Gold Bluffs Beach trailhead
Distance: 3.3-mile one way
Hiking time: About 3 hours
Difficulty: Easy
Elevation gain: 25 feet
Trail surface: Dirt and sand/beach
Hours open: 24 hours
Best season: Late spring to early autumn
Water: At the trailhead
Toilets: At the trailhead
Nursing benches: Picnic tables at the trailhead
Stroller-friendly: No
Potential child hazards: None

Other trail users: None
Dogs: Not allowed
Land status: California Department of Parks and Recreation
Nearest town: Orick
Fees and permits: Day-use fee
Maps: Prairie Creek Redwoods State Park brochure
Trail contact: Prairie Creek Redwoods State Park, 127011 Newton B. Drury Scenic Pkwy., Orick, CA 95555; (707) 488-2039; www.parks.ca.gov/?page_id=415
Gear suggestions: Sturdy shoes and sand toys

FINDING THE TRAILHEAD

From Redding, take CA 299 west for approximately 135 miles. Take the exit onto US 101 north toward Crescent City and go 35 miles. Turn left onto Davison Road and go 3.7 miles until it turns into Gold Bluffs Beach E Road. Stay on that road for another 2 miles and then turn left into the Gold Bluffs Beach Picnic Area. There is usually plenty of parking. GPS: N41 23.01' / W124 4.17'

THE HIKE

Getting to the trailhead itself can be as much of an adventure as the actual hiking. Unpaved Davison Road can be a breeze, or sometimes you may be dodging potholes and wondering if your sedan is going to survive the return trip. Be extra careful fording some of the streams that run across the road; although not particularly deep, they can hide some dropoffs that will give your car's undercarriage an unnecessary love tap.

After driving the 7 miles from the paved area, you'll pass the Gold Bluffs campground. As an alternative you can park in this day-use area, and then head due west toward the sound of the surf. The map depicts driving another 1.5 miles north so you can share a parking lot with the Fern Canyon hike and easily pair these together; parking at either

One of the herds of resident Roosevelt elk grazing on the prairie

Much of the hike is spent playing tag with the surf.

end will not make a difference, although the Fern Canyon lot can be slightly more crowded on prime weekends.

About the only major landmark along the way are the eponymous Gold Bluffs on your left as you make your way south, which add a beautifully rich hue to the greens and blues of the coast. Otherwise this is a straightforward hike in the sand, and with hardly any navigation to worry about, it's a great introductory hike for the family (especially if paired up with the Fern Canyon hike). If you'd like to improve your chances of seeing any elk, your best bet is to hike along the dunes (although it's twice the workout in the soft sand), as the beach drops toward the coastline and otherwise obscures your view onto the grassland. Please make sure to stay off the grasslands themselves, as trampling them can destroy important food sources for the variety of wildlife in the area.

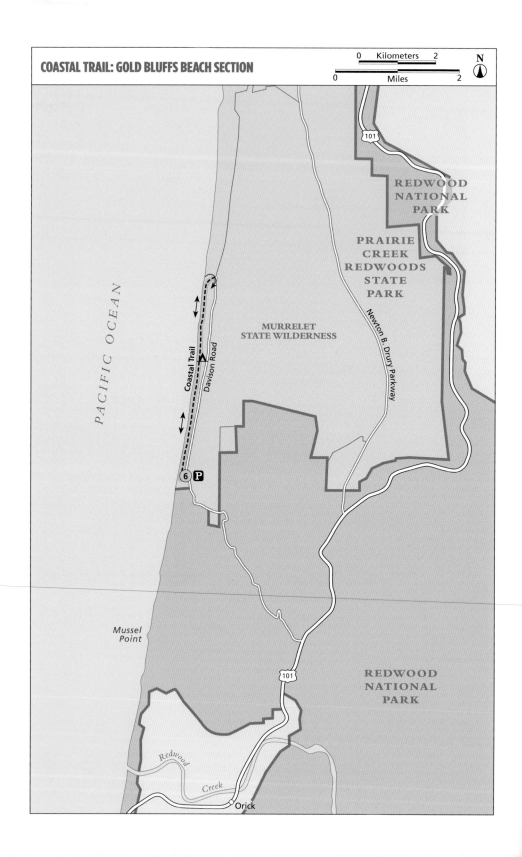

0   Kilometers   2

0   Miles   2

N

PACIFIC OCEAN

REDWOOD
NATIONAL
PARK

PRAIRIE
CREEK
REDWOODS
STATE
PARK

MURRELET
STATE WILDERNESS

Newton B. Drury Parkway

Coastal Trail

Davison Road

101

6   P

Mussel
Point

101

REDWOOD
NATIONAL
PARK

Redwood

Creek

Orick

The famed Gold Bluffs that give this section its name

A little over 100 years ago, there were even California grizzly bears who likely hunted in this area. Before the gold rush, there are estimates of up to 10,000 grizzly bears in the state, and they were some of the largest of their species because they could hunt year-round. Today only black bears are found in the park, but it's unlikely you'll see one on this particular hike. If you time your hike during the spring season (usually April to May), there's a fairly good chance you'll also see humpback whales as they migrate with the calves from the warm Baja waters to farther north. Look for the spouts along the horizon, and you may get lucky and see a tail fluke as well.

MILES AND DIRECTIONS

0.0 Begin the hike by heading due west from the parking area toward the ocean.

0.05 Once you hit the beach, turn right. You'll follow the beach all the way north until you reach the opposite end at Fern Canyon.

1.2 Pass the turnoff to the right that goes to the Beach Campground.

3.3 You've reached the end of the trail. Catch a shuttle back to the beginning or retrace your steps for double the mileage.

FUN FACTOR: GO LONG WITH THE ENTIRE CCT

This short segment represents just 1.5 miles of the 70-mile Coastal Trail within Redwood National Park. The trail is almost end-to-end in the backcountry, save one major detour over the Klamath River on US 101. You can access it from several points (like this one), and you can string together an incredible multi-night trip if your family is at that level of backpacking. This trail is also part of the planned 1,200-mile California Coastal Trail (CCT). Although still a long ways from completion, this section and those in the surrounding counties are some of the better sections at this stage of development.

7 COLLEGE COVE TRAIL

In a state that's famous for its beaches, it's nice to know you can still find easy beach access without any crowds. This pairs very nicely with the Elk Head Trail; they depart from the same trailhead, and you can feasibly complete the Elk Head hike and then come down to College Cove for an afternoon exploring the beach and tidepools. Try to time it with low tide, as you'll have access to hike around the corner to the main Trinidad State Beach. Pro tip: Bring water shoes for you and your kids, as some of the tidepool areas have sharp rocks, but there's enough water that standard boots will get soaked.

Start: Elk Head trailhead
Distance: 0.5-mile round-trip
Hiking time: About 1 hour
Difficulty: Easy
Elevation gain: 122 feet
Trail surface: Dirt and sand
Hours open: Sunrise to sunset
Best season: Late spring to early autumn (low tide is the best time to visit)
Water: None
Toilets: At the trailhead
Nursing benches: Tables in the small picnic area
Stroller-friendly: No

Potential child hazards: None
Other trail users: None
Dogs: Not allowed on trails
Land status: California Department of Parks and Recreation
Nearest town: Trinidad
Fees and permits: Fee
Maps: Trinidad State Beach map
Trail contact: Trinidad State Beach, 4150 Patrick's Point Dr.; (707) 677-3570; https://www.parks.ca .gov/?page_id=418
Gear suggestions: Sturdy shoes and sand toys

FINDING THE TRAILHEAD

From Redding, take CA 299 west for approximately 135 miles. Take the exit onto US 101 north toward Crescent City and go 13 miles. Take exit 728 for Trinidad and then turn left onto Main Street. Immediately after passing under the highway, turn right onto Patrick's Point Drive and go 0.5 mile. Turn left onto Anderson Lane and then right onto Stagecoach Road. The entrance to the state beach will be on your left. Parking is limited and busy on summer weekends. GPS: N41 4.13' / W124 9.16'

THE HIKE

Start from the Elk Head Trail parking lot and make your way down the heavily wooded path. After about 1,000 feet you'll see a path that cuts down toward a beach. This is your turn, and certainly the trickiest part of the hike. There are crude steps built into the path, but take your time, especially if you have a child in a pack on your back. Once you descend about 120 feet, you'll arrive at the northwestern end of the beautifully shaped College Cove Beach, which arcs away from you toward the town of Trinidad. This beach is nicely protected and it's easy to find a spot to set up basecamp while your kids go explore. If you have the gumption, consider walking 10 minutes away from where the trail comes out as you'll have more privacy the farther you go down the beach.

The start of the trail shrouded in ocean mist and tree cover

Once you've set up shop, continue hiking to explore all the natural features in the area. There are seasonal waterfalls (small ones, they're more like cascades), and if you've timed low tide well, you can head south/southeast to connect to the more popular Trinidad State Beach. If you can get your kids to sit still by the tidepool, you'll see dozens of creatures emerge from hiding and go about their daily routine. Most common are barnacles, sea anemones, sea stars, kelp, and all sorts of crabs. If the tide is particularly low, you can wade through The Portal, which is a natural sea arch tucked around the corner on the way to the main state beach.

Pewetole Island (peh-WEH-toll, the native Tsurai name for the rock) is one of the largest sea stacks in the area, and at 130 feet tall it makes an obvious landmark between College Cove and Trinidad State Beach. This was the former edge of the sea cliffs, but after years of water broke down the weaker parts of the cliff, they eventually eroded and

FUN FACTOR: SEND THE KIDS TO COLLEGE

For more education masked as fun, consider going to the 50+-year-old Humboldt State University Telonicher Marine Lab in the town of Trinidad. There's a low-cost tour through seven aquariums and touch tanks (much more recommended than having your kids do a DIY touch tank on the beach). You can also sign up for a guided tidepool tour. Finally, you can register for a virtual Marine Science Summer Camp for kids in first through sixth grades, and you'll receive a week's worth of programming like experiments, craft projects, and interviews with researchers.

Looking toward Pewetole Island on a moody coastal morning

One of the many tidepools to explore at low tide

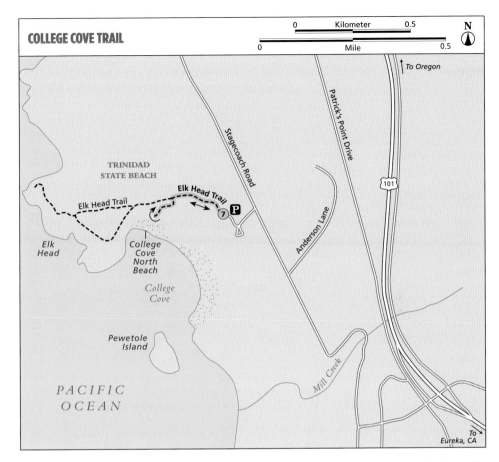

left the sea stack standing alone. There's a collection of Sitka spruce perched on the island, and annually seabirds like black oystercatchers will return to build their nests in the vegetation.

MILES AND DIRECTIONS

0.0   Start at the Elk Head trailhead.

0.1   Take the left trail toward College Cove North beach.

0.25 Arrive at College Cove North beach.

0.5   Arrive back at the trailhead.

8 DRURY-CHANEY LOOP TRAIL

Picture a verdant green understory with mighty trees soaring impossibly high into the sky and sprinkled with dappled sunlight that twinkles gently as it filters toward the forest floor. That's the reality in the picturesque Drury-Chaney Trail, a mystical loop that inspires a bit of magic in all of us.

Start: Drury-Chaney trailhead
Distance: 2.4-mile lollipop loop
Hiking time: About 1.5 hours
Difficulty: Easy
Elevation gain: 30 feet
Trail surface: Dirt and woodchip
Hours open: 24 hours
Best season: Any season
Water: None
Toilets: None
Nursing benches: None
Stroller-friendly: No
Potential child hazards: None
Other trail users: None

Dogs: Not allowed
Land status: California Department of Parks and Recreation
Nearest town: Redcrest
Fees and permits: Day-use fee
Maps: Humboldt Redwoods State Park brochure
Trail contact: Humboldt Redwoods State Park, 17119 Avenue of the Giants, Weott, CA 95571; (707) 946-2263; www.parks.ca.gov/?page_id=425
Gear suggestions: Sturdy shoes

FINDING THE TRAILHEAD

From Redding, take I-5 south for approximately 16 miles and take exit 662 for Bowman Road. Travel for 14 miles and then turn right onto CA 36 west and go 118 miles. Turn left to merge onto US 101 south and go 14 miles to exit 671 toward Holmes/Redcrest. Take a left at the end of the ramp onto Barkdull Road and then a quick left onto CA 254 north (aka Avenue of the Giants). Parking is a half-mile ahead on either side of the road. Parking is limited and you must ensure your car is completely within the white lines and does not block traffic.
GPS: N40 26.58' / W123 59.18'

THE HIKE

Walking into the forest of the Drury-Chaney Trail almost feels like walking into a library. Once you step beneath the canopy of needles high above you, a reverent silence descends, filling the air with the thick sound of nothingness. It's so peaceful, in fact, that we found ourselves shushing our daughter as she raced ahead on the perfectly flat trail as it wound toward the base of a gargantuan tree.

Of course, peace and quiet are always nice, but the hiking trail brings a lot of magic to the younger group too. Powerful redwoods feel inconceivably large to small children as their necks crank backward and their eyes lift so far into the sky that they can't actually see where the treetops end. A few downed trunks lay perpendicular to the trail with a girth so massive that we were able to walk two abreast as we danced across the makeshift balance beam.

Yes, this loop is definitely one to check out. It's shaped like a lollipop split into three equal sections: 0.8 mile for the approach (or the lollipop stick), 0.8 mile for the loop (or the lollipop itself), and the return 0.8 mile back down.

The start of the grove just as we departed the trailhead

Begin your hike at the parking lot on Avenue of the Giants, the main scenic highway that runs through Humboldt Redwoods State Park. You'll see a sign for the town of Pepperwood (population: 50); that's how you know you're in the right spot.

Almost immediately, the trail enters a supernatural world of dense jungle and thick green carpet. Both the Eel River across Avenue of the Giants and the entire Eel River Valley seem to act as a highway for coastal mist wafting in from the ocean. With it

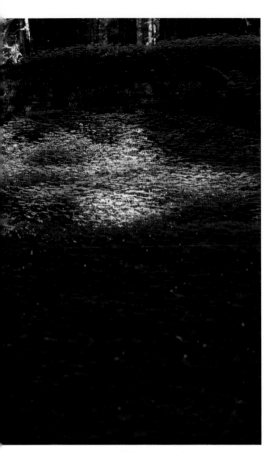

One of the beautiful carpets of redwood sorrel

comes heavy moisture that creates the perfect environment for ferns and sorrel, a bright green leafy groundcover. In the first quarter-mile of this trail, the sorrel is so dense that it looks like the redwoods are protruding through a wrinkled, green carpet that covers the forest floor. In a word, it's awesome.

Pass the pair of picnic tables on the small patch of grass before taking a left and entering the forest. You'll traverse along the base of a grove of redwoods to your left, immediately reminding you of how small we actually are. While you and the kids are only a few feet from the parking lot, it will feel like you've entered an alternate reality.

Continue heading due west, as you will do for the entirety of the first 0.8-mile section. This first leg is where the sorrel and ferns shine against the redwoods above, so take a moment to enjoy the scenery. Many of the trees in this stretch are younger, but there are still some giants in the mix. At 0.5 mile, you'll notice a bench chopped into a log on the left side of the trail. If you have tired little legs, this is a great place to rest and ponder at the majesty surrounding you.

At 0.65 mile, you'll come to an intersection with a dirt road labeled "Gated Park Access Trail." Continue straight to stay on the Drury-Chaney Trail.

FUN FACTOR: WHY DO BIG TREES HAVE SUCH SHALLOW ROOTS?

Redwoods may reach to the heavens, but their root system is anything but deep. These leviathans believe in community. Most redwood roots are only 5 or 6 feet deep, which is certainly not enough to anchor them to the earth. However, they make up for their lack of depth with their intertwined sprawl that stretches up to 100 feet away from the trunk. In fact, the roots often stretch toward other tree roots, latching together and eventually fusing into one, as if the trees are holding on to each other for support. This unified approach protects the trees from predators and attacks by Mother Nature while also enabling the trees to take in more nutrients that seep in from the soil.

DRURY-CHANEY LOOP TRAIL

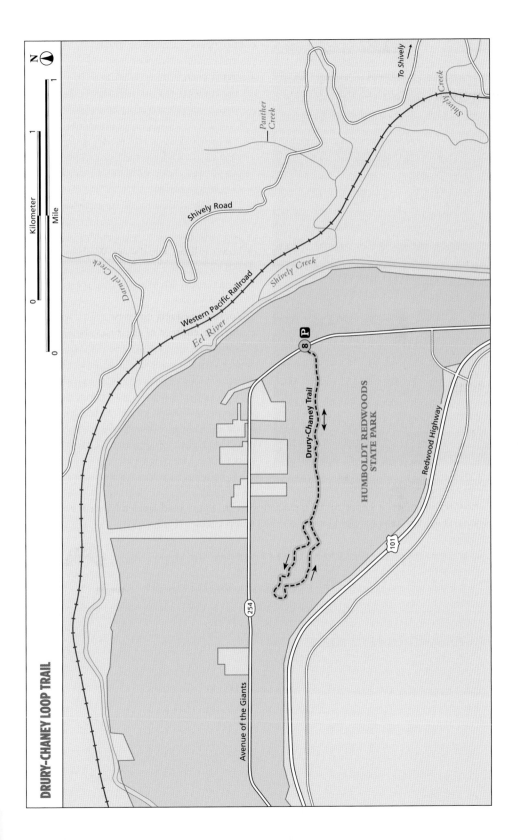

It's a fine balance between free exploration and making sure there's some self-preservation.

Just before you arrive at the start of the 0.8-mile loop portion of the hike, you'll notice a magnificent downed redwood on the left side of the trail. Now fallen, the tree's monstrous roots are exposed and provide an excellent spot for a quick chat with the kids in the group to help them understand how the gigantic redwoods actually have shallow root structures (see sidebar).

Almost immediately afterward, you'll come to the loop portion, identified with a basic sign that says "Loop Trail." There are no trail junctions on the Loop Trail, so you can go in either direction and end up back at this spot. For the sake of these directions, we'll go in a counterclockwise direction, so start by turning right.

A dense layer of ferns is particularly noticeable in this piece of trail, but don't forget to look up and admire some of the larger redwoods in this area. Coastal redwoods can often live up to 2,000 years, and some of the older trees in this hike are thought to be anywhere from 800 to 1,500 years old. Talk about longevity!

Continue along the path, passing by a few benches as you wrap through the sea of giant trees. At just over 0.5 mile into the loop, you'll reach the first of two wooden bridges. This first bridge is the longest and makes for a good spot for family photos.

You'll reach the second, shorter bridge just before you arrive back at the approach leg of the trail that brought you to the loop. Close the loop before turning right and heading back the way you came. Once again, you'll encounter the dirt road intersection 0.15 mile after the loop. Stay straight and return to Avenue of the Giants.

MILES AND DIRECTIONS

0.0   Begin at the marked trailhead on the east side of Avenue of the Giants.

0.65 Trail intersection; stay straight.

0.8   Trail junction; turn right and begin the loop portion of the hike.

1.3   Cross the wooden bridge.

1.65 Trail junction; turn left and close the loop section. Then, stay straight and retrace your steps back to the car.

2.4   Arrive back at the car.

9 ELK HEAD TRAIL

This short trail is a hidden gem on the California coast. Not only is it a perfect stopover to stretch your legs in the middle of a longer trip, but it's also a wonderful destination in its own right. The charming seaside town of Trinidad has plenty of local spots for stocking up on treats (whether for adults or children), and the slow pace can be a welcome respite if you're coming from a more urban area. The hike is largely quiet, and the views up and down the coast make for a fitting reward, especially given the nominal effort.

Start: Elk Head trailhead
Distance: 1.4-mile out-and-back
Hiking time: 1.5 to 2 hours
Difficulty: Easy
Elevation gain: 134 feet
Trail surface: Dirt and rock
Hours open: Sunrise to sunset
Best season: Late spring to early autumn (low tide is the best time to visit)
Water: None
Toilets: At the trailhead
Nursing benches: Tables in the small picnic area

Stroller-friendly: No
Potential child hazards: None
Other trail users: None
Dogs: Not allowed on trails
Land status: California Department of Parks and Recreation
Nearest town: Trinidad
Fees and permits: Fee
Maps: Trinidad State Beach map
Trail contact: Trinidad State Beach, 4150 Patrick's Point Dr.; (707) 677-3570; https://www.parks.ca .gov/?page_id=418
Gear suggestions: Sturdy shoes

FINDING THE TRAILHEAD

From Redding, take CA 299 west for approximately 135 miles. Take the exit onto US 101 north toward Crescent City and go 13 miles. Take exit 728 for Trinidad and then turn left onto Main Street. Immediately after passing under the highway, turn right onto Patrick's Point Drive for 0.5 mile. Turn left onto Anderson Lane and then right onto Stagecoach Road. The entrance to the state beach will be on your left. Parking is limited and busy on summer weekends.
GPS: N41 4.07' / W124 9.49'

THE HIKE

Because this is mostly off the radar, it can be hard to find information or even the right trailhead. That's exactly what happened to us when looking for the parking lot, but eventually we found it tucked off of Stagecoach Road headed out of town. The start of the hike is mostly treed and slightly downhill, and you can tell the local greenery benefits from the high levels of year-round moisture. As you make your way through the rich alder forest, after about 1,000 feet you'll see the split for the trail down to College Cove Beach; continue west toward Elk Head. Just ahead you'll come to another unmarked split; although going straight will get you to the final destination a little faster, it's worth taking the left route to Omenoku Point and a nice southern-facing overlook toward Trinidad Head. From this point the trail turns northwest, and after about 500 feet you'll rejoin the connector trail you passed earlier and head toward Megwil Point.

Top: Looking down the trail as you approach Megwil Point
Left: One of the early views to the west as you cross to the far side of Elk Head
Right: Looking north from Megwil Point

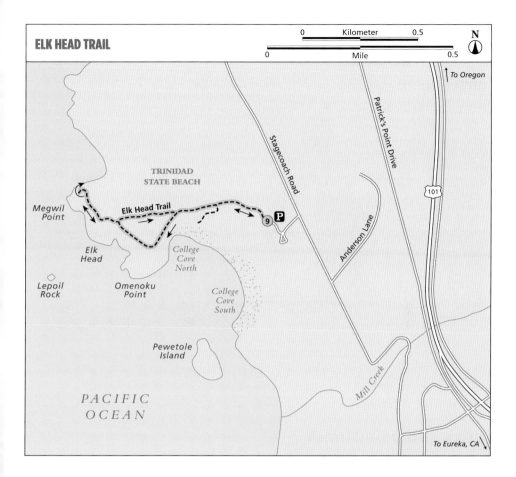

ELK HEAD TRAIL

0   Kilometer   0.5

0   Mile   0.5

N

To Oregon

Patrick's Point Drive

Stagecoach Road

TRINIDAD
STATE BEACH

Elk Head Trail

101

Megwil
Point

Anderson Lane

Elk
Head

College
Cove
North

Lepoil
Rock

Omenoku
Point

College
Cove
South

Pewetole
Island

PACIFIC
OCEAN

Mill Creek

To Eureka, CA

Once you pass this junction and the horse-prevention gate, the trail begins to open up and you start to get views toward the Pacific. If you time it right during wildflower season, you'll find a wild variety of colors and shapes along the trail, and we'll frequently start a contest with our daughter to see who can find the largest variety of wildflowers (winner gets to pick where we get dessert back in town). We readily admit this is a ploy to get her to run ahead on the trail so she can find them first, but whatever keeps the day fun seems to be well worth it.

Midsummer wildflower bloom

Walk down the stairs to get out onto Megwil Point proper, and if you have young children (or daredevil partners), keep a close eye on them to make sure they stay back from the edge. This is rugged, untrammeled coastline that likely feels similar to the way

it did hundreds of years ago, and just as it was then, there are no safety nets. There are a few safe places to set up a small picnic and keep an eye out for dolphins, whales, sea lions, and any number of seabirds, so plan to spend some time out on the point before retracing your steps back to the car.

MILES AND DIRECTIONS

0.0 Find the path that leaves from the south side of the parking lot.

0.2 Trail split: You can go either direction and you'll still end up in the same place.

0.5 The trail merges back together just prior to descending toward the beach.

0.7 You've reached the beach. Turn around and retrace your steps back to the car.

1.4 Arrive back at the car.

10 FERN CANYON LOOP TRAIL

With towering canyon walls covered in ancient ferns and dripping glittering droplets of moisture, it's easy to see why Fern Canyon is often mistaken for a fairyland. But this mystical place is very real, and it's the perfect location for your family's next adventure.

Start: Fern Canyon Car Park
Distance: 1.0-mile lollipop loop
Hiking time: About 1 hour
Difficulty: Easy
Elevation gain: 118 feet
Trail surface: Dirt and streambed
Hours open: 24 hours
Best season: Late spring to early autumn
Water: In the campground
Toilets: At the parking lot
Nursing benches: Picnic tables at the trailhead
Stroller-friendly: No
Potential child hazards: Stream crossings

Other trail users: None
Dogs: Not allowed
Land status: California Department of Parks and Recreation
Nearest town: Orick
Fees and permits: Day-use fee
Maps: Prairie Creek Redwoods State Park brochure
Trail contact: Prairie Creek Redwoods State Park, 127011 Newton B. Drury Scenic Pkwy., Orick, CA 95555; (707) 488-2039; www.parks .ca.gov/?page_id=415
Gear suggestions: Sturdy shoes

FINDING THE TRAILHEAD

From Redding, take CA 299 west for approximately 135 miles. Take the exit onto US 101 north toward Crescent City and go 35 miles. Turn left onto Davison Road. Follow the scenic road for 6 miles until you reach the Gold Bluffs Beach kiosk. The trailhead starts at the Fern Canyon Car Park. GPS: N41 24.09' / W124 3.9'

THE HIKE

When Steven Spielberg directed the movie *Jurassic Park 2: The Lost World*, he chose Fern Canyon as one of the filming sites thanks to its reputation as an "unforgettable natural wonder." We're certainly not filmmakers or experts in cinematography, but we figure that Steven sees a lot of beautiful places in this world. If he thinks Fern Canyon is one of the most awe-inspiring trails, we suspect you'll feel the same.

We sure did!

But before you even set out for the trailhead, be sure to visit the National Park Service website to double-check that Fern Canyon is ready for visitors. The windy and long gravel road that travels to the trailhead often sees its share of potholes. During rainy months, the potholes can fill or other sections of the road can wash out, so it's a good idea to verify accessibility before venturing to this trail.

Speaking of rain, it's also best to prepare yourself and the kids for wet hiking conditions. From June through September, park rangers typically install wooden pedestrian bridges that cross the wettest areas of the canyon, but there is still a lot of splashing. It all adds to the fun—and kids love it!—but you definitely want to know before you go.

Crossing one of the low bridges at the mouth of the canyon

Hiking toward the first bend in the trail

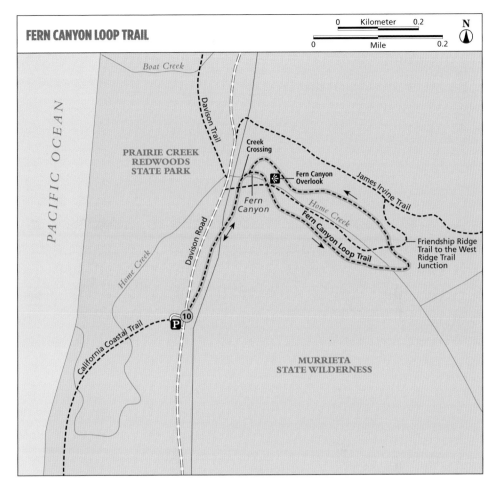

Once you reach the parking lot, however, you'll quickly realize that Fern Canyon is arguably one of the best kid-friendly trails in the state. The parking lot is large and features a few picnic tables alongside a restroom for last-minute bathroom breaks. Once you're done there, head over to the obvious dirt path in the corner. This is the approach trail that takes you directly to the canyon.

The real highlight of Fern Canyon is the accessibility. The dirt approach path is a quick quarter-mile walk that lasts just a few minutes before dumping you at the entrance to the canyon itself. Our daughter (who was 3 years old) knew this trail led to the good stuff, so she eagerly ran the entire thing in anticipation for what was to come.

And she *definitely* wasn't disappointed.

After the quarter-mile, the trail splits and you will see a sign that identifies the James Irvine Trail to the left. Stay to the right. You'll be following alongside a cobbled stream called Home Creek as it winds and wraps throughout the canyon floor. In places, the water seeps out of its containment, so you have no choice but to walk through a few inches of moisture. As a result, you'll often see hikers carrying their shoes or otherwise trying to stay dry, but here's a pro tip: Embrace it. If you and your family spend all your time worrying about wet feet, you'll miss the best part: the scenery!

Endless exploration in a nice walled trail—perfect for kids who want to run!

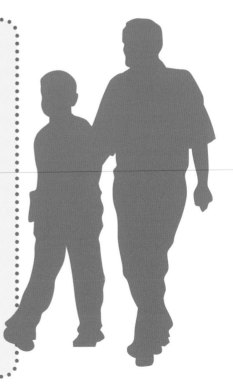

FUN FACTOR: SPOT THE ROOSEVELT ELK

While Fern Canyon may conjure images of dinosaurs and twinkling fairies, the Roosevelt elk are the highlight of the animal kingdom in the Pacific Northwest, with some spreading as far south as Northern California. Known as the largest members of the deer family, the elk are considered to be a wildly successful conservation story after they were hunted to near-extinction by North Coast settlers. Conservation efforts ramped up when there were only a few hundred elk left. In fact, many believe that the elk were a driving force behind President Theodore Roosevelt's establishment of Washington's Mount Olympus National Monument in 1909. Today, there are thousands of Roosevelt spread through the Pacific Northwest and Northern California, with a small population living in Prairie Creek Redwoods State Park. The elk can be viewed at two locations: Elk Prairie on the Newton Drury Scenic Highway, and Elk Meadow, just off US 101 on Davison Road, the same road you'll take to the Fern Canyon trailhead.

After crossing the first pedestrian bridge, the 50-foot canyon walls begin to rise up around you, densely covered in lush vegetation. The secret to the plant life is the excessive moisture and minimal sunshine. There is no other way to say it: The walls are wall-to-wall covered (see what we did there?) in ancient ferns that thrive in these growing conditions. In fact, there are more than five types of ferns sprawling around the canyon with verdant moss filling in between the gaps.

As you venture deeper into the canyon, you'll continue to cross over small board bridges and walk through various pools of cool, clear water. It doesn't matter whether your children are 3 or 13; this type of terrain is a party. Eventually, your family will notice a few downed trees that make for a great natural playground.

Near the back, tiny waterfalls trickle down the canyon walls as moisture gently drips from the fern leaves. It's a fun kid activity to watch the droplets venture down the wall before disappearing into the trickling stream at their feet. Our daughter enjoyed trying to catch a few on her tongue!

Our daughter counting the leaves on the fern-covered walls

Once you reach the back of the canyon, you'll notice a staircase that climbs up to the top of the walls. If you wish, you can ascend the trail here and turn left. This is the loop trail that meanders along the canyon rim before depositing you back at the beginning.

Or, if your kids enjoyed their first pass through the canyon, you can always do what we did: Forgo the staircase, turn around, and walk back through the magical fairy forest that is Fern Canyon.

MILES AND DIRECTIONS

0.0 From the parking area, find the paved, multiuse trail on the northeast corner of the parking lot, and head that way.

0.2 Pass a bench that affords a stunning view of the ocean.

0.25 Turn right and head into the canyon.

0.5 You've reached the back of the canyon. Turn around and retrace your steps back to the trailhead, or take the stairs and make a loop.

1.0 Arrive back at the trailhead.

11 KINGS CREEK FALLS

Hiking is often about the journey, not the destination. That mantra is apparent in this hike where beautiful scenery along the trail visually trumps the waterfall at the end. Nevertheless, anyone who has visited the famous Yosemite Falls will notice the similarities to Kings Creek—only with a fraction of the crowds.

Start: Kings Creek Falls trailhead
Distance: 2.7-mile loop
Hiking time: About 2 hours
Difficulty: Moderate
Elevation gain: 486 feet (most of which is a steep, narrow stone staircase)
Trail surface: Dirt and rock
Hours open: Open daily, 24 hours a day, but the road to the trailhead is closed approximately from Nov until June depending on snow
Best season: Late spring to early autumn
Water: Fill up at any of the visitor centers
Toilets: At the trailhead
Nursing benches: No
Stroller-friendly: No

Potential child hazards: Steep ledges and narrow stone stairs at the Cascades Foot Trail, bear habitat, and several stream crossings
Other trail users: None
Dogs: Not allowed
Land status: National Park Service
Nearest town: Mineral
Fees and permits: Fee to enter the park, or purchase America the Beautiful annual pass
Maps: Lassen Volcanic National Park map
Trail contact: Lassen Volcanic National Park, PO Box 100, Mineral, CA 96063; (530) 595-4480; www.nps.gov/lavo
Gear suggestions: Trekking poles and water shoes

FINDING THE TRAILHEAD

From Redding, take CA 44 east for approximately 47 miles. Turn right to head south on CA 89 toward the park entrance. After 15 miles, pull off to the side of the road (the trailhead is on the left). Parking is extremely limited on the side of the road. Make sure your car is not blocking the road and completely within the white lines. Do not park on the grass. GPS: N40 27.62' / W121 27.58'

THE HIKE

There is a reason visitors often see a yellow school bus parked at this trailhead: Kids love Kings Creek! It's a popular hike for schools in the area. As a result, don't expect much solitude, but what would you expect from one of the best hikes in Lassen National Park?

The trailhead is located on the south side of CA 89, but there isn't a lot of space and most available spots are in dirt turnouts on the side of the road. As a result, you'll likely spot the correct trailhead when you notice a series of cars lining the highway. Note: There are no restrooms at this trailhead either, so plan accordingly.

The soft dirt path begins with an initial mellow descent through a dense grove of fir trees with Kings Creek itself babbling along the right side. But at a quarter-mile, you'll leave the forest and begin traversing along the edge of Lower Kings Creek Meadow. If you time it right and visit during the late spring or early summer, this makes for a stunning view as the verdant green grass is often peppered with wildly colorful corn lilies.

One of the early meadow crossings as you head down the canyon

Remember this resting spot for your return trip: It makes for a great reprieve on the uphill. But until then, continue alongside the meadow until you reach a trail junction at roughly 0.7 mile.

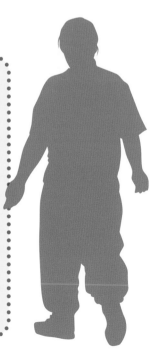

FUN FACTOR: SPLASH IN THE SUN

It doesn't matter if you have swimsuits or dirty hiking clothes that are damp with sweat from your return hike back from the falls. If you have extra time, consider a play session in Kings Creek. As you descend from the trailhead during the first few steps of the Kings Creek Falls hike, you'll immediately notice Kings Creek itself running along your right side. Cut through the dirt patch and set up a veritable picnic in the shade next to the babbling water. Later in the summer, low water levels mean safety isn't an issue. On our recent July trip, our 3-year-old could easily splash around without much concern. Bonus: If you're extra prepared, stash a few water squirters or buckets in your car. Not only will your kids have a blast in the refreshing water, but you'll be able to log a few minutes of utter relaxation in Mother Nature. Perfection.

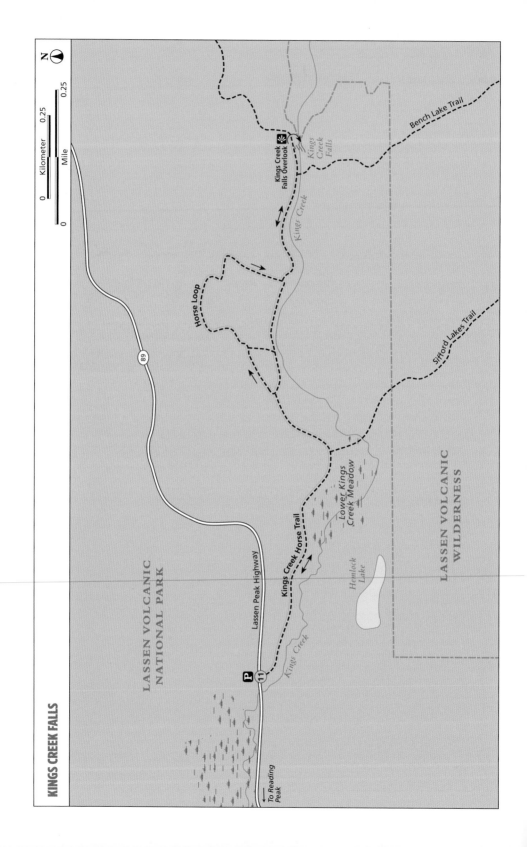

KINGS CREEK FALLS

N

Kilometer
0   0.25

Mile
0   0.25

LASSEN VOLCANIC
NATIONAL PARK

Lassen Peak Highway

89

11

P

To Reading
Peak

Kings Creek

Kings Creek Horse Trail

Hemlock
Lake

Lower Kings
Creek Meadow

Horse Loop

Kings Creek

Kings Creek
Falls Overlook

Kings
Creek
Falls

Bench Lake Trail

Sifford Lakes Trail

LASSEN VOLCANIC
WILDERNESS

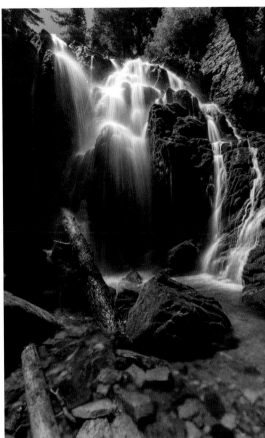

Left: View of the falls from the overlook
Right: Looking up from the pool at the base of the falls

Here, you have a choice, but you'll notice the trail to the right is identified as a one-way route. That's the way you'll return, so stay to the left. The trail steeply descends for a half-mile on steps carved into the rock. The trail journeys through an area known as the Upper Cascades, aptly named for the expansive views as you steadily hike downhill. For those who have visited Yosemite Falls via the Mist Trail in Yosemite National Park, this section of Kings Creek will likely feel familiar. The vantage points of the surrounding scenery and granite stairs are similar, although this hike is significantly less steep.

At 1.2 miles, turn left as you merge back onto the final leg of the trail, continuing downhill alongside the rushing foam-capped water while hiking along the creek itself. It's not uncommon for hikers to admire the various cascades along this section trail and assume they've made it to the big show. But unless you've arrived at the fenced overlook, keep hiking.

At 1.4 miles, you'll reach the fenced overlook and know that you've arrived at Kings Creek Falls. The 40-foot-tall waterfall drips down a series of large boulders and the misty-cool air feels refreshing on hot summer days. Be sure to stick around here until all the little legs are rested. Remember how the kids scampered through the downhill? Now it's time to go up!

Hiking back up the Foot Trail option past the Cascades

Climb the steep, narrow stairs back uphill, staying to the left to return on the one-way foot trail you spotted earlier. You'll regain more than 700 feet in elevation, so slow and steady is the best way to go.

When you arrive back at the meadows, we highly recommend plopping down in the shade and enjoying a snack break. You only have a half-mile or so left, but all of the climbing is done so take a minute to relax and soak in the views.

MILES AND DIRECTIONS

0.0   Begin hiking at the signed Kings Creek Falls Trailhead on the south side of Lassen Peak Highway.

0.25   Leave the forest and begin traversing alongside Lower Kings Creek Meadow.

0.7   Trail junction; stay left.

1.2   Hike past the Upper Cascades but continue onward; you aren't at the falls yet!

1.4   Arrive at the fenced overlook for Kings Creek Falls. Once you're done admiring the water, turn around and climb the steep staircase away from the waterfall.

1.8   Trail junction; stay left.

2.2   Traverse alongside Lower Kings Creek Meadow once more.

2.7   Arrive back at the trailhead.

12 LADY BIRD JOHNSON GROVE

The level, short hike is a great introduction to the redwoods. It's one of the first locations you hit—since most hikers will arrive from the south—so it's a good appetizer for bigger groves down the road. If it's at all possible to get here early in the morning (we know that could be a tall order depending on the age of your kids), the solitude and low-angle light make this place extra serene.

Start: Lady Bird Johnson Grove trailhead
Distance: 1.3-mile lollipop loop
Hiking time: About 1 hour
Difficulty: Easy
Elevation gain: 75 feet
Trail surface: Dirt
Hours open: Open daily, 24 hours a day
Best season: Spring to autumn
Water: At any of the visitor centers
Toilets: At the trailhead
Nursing benches: No
Stroller-friendly: Yes
Potential child hazards: Poison oak along the trail edges and abundant amount of ticks

Other trail users: None
Dogs: Not allowed
Land status: National Park Service
Nearest town: Orick
Fees and permits: None
Maps: Redwood National and State Park map
Trail contact: Redwood National and State Park, 1111 Second St., Crescent City, CA 95531; (707) 464-6101; https://www.nps.gov/redw
Gear suggestions: Sturdy shoes and gaiters (the ferns along the trail are always wet)

FINDING THE TRAILHEAD

From Redding, take CA 299 west for approximately 135 miles. Take the exit toward Crescent City and stay on US 101 north for approximately 34 miles. Turn right onto Bald Hills Road for 2.6 miles until you reach the trailhead parking on your right. Parking is extremely limited, and this is one of the busiest trailheads in the park. GPS: N41 18.21' / W124 1.09'

THE HIKE

The Lady Bird Johnson Trail is special since the grove is situated on a ridgeline 1,200 feet above sea level. This means it feels different than other lower groves, largely thanks to the open vegetation that also makes it easier to see the full height of the trees.

The government initially dedicated this grove in 1969, and the footbridge that connects the parking lot to the main trail feels like it's straight from the same era. If you search for photos of this hike you'll find the bridge is a frequent star, as the coloring and shape stand out from the surrounding vegetation in a memorable way. If you time it right, you can catch pockets of sunlight dropping down onto the bridge, beckoning you across like a portal to another world.

Once you've crossed over Bald Hills Road, continue for about a third of a mile until you get to the start of the lollipop loop. Continuing straight will keep you with the flow of foot traffic, and it will also build the interest as the grove gets better and better when hiked in a clockwise direction. This initial section is rife with huckleberry; continue onward to get to the good stuff.

The soft trail floor makes for comfortable hiking.

Morning sunlight filters through grove

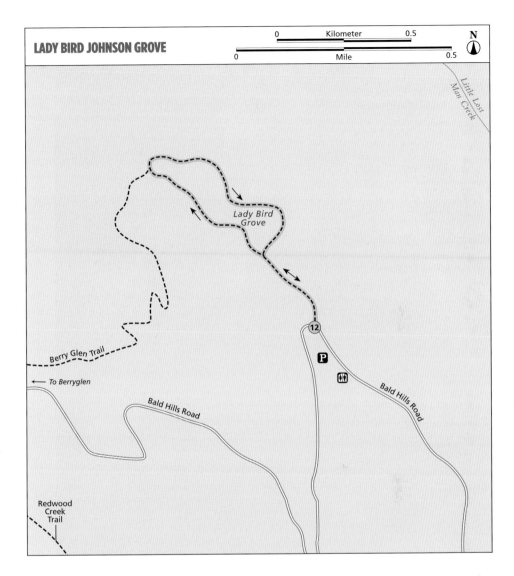

0   Kilometer   0.5

0   Mile   0.5

N

Little Lost Man Creek

Lady Bird Grove

12

Berry Glen Trail

← To Berryglen

Bald Hills Road

Bald Hills Road

Redwood Creek Trail

Walk another third of a mile past the intersection and you'll come to the Berry Glen Trail junction. If your family is looking for a longer hike, this relatively new connector trail runs 3 miles downhill to the Elk Meadow area, and given the consistent downhill grade, it can be a little easier for small legs (assuming you can run a car shuttle, of course). There are not too many views beyond the forest, but the trail itself is very well maintained and makes for a pleasant stroll. If you want to do this as a loop from the Elk Meadow area, the total walk (plus the Lady Bird Johnson Grove loop described here) is about 7 miles.

Just past the Berry Glen Trail junction comes the dedication site where President Nixon presided over the ceremony back in 1969. Take a minute to read the plaque and relax on the bench, as from this moment on the trail gets better and better. Continue tracking the trail as it loops through bigger and bigger redwoods, and if you're present in

Looking up toward one of the mammoths at a clearing along the trail

the spring you'll see the classic rhododendron blooms punctuating the green understory with their pinkish hues.

Because this is an upland grove, you're also more likely to be enshrouded in clouds than in some of the lower groves, which makes for moody hiking and the potential for incredible light shows. At either end of the day you can catch crepuscular rays shining through the fog and trees, and the light can shift minute by minute to completely change the feel of the scenery. Even though it's a short hike, it's easy to lose an hour or two here.

Rhododendron blooms decorate the trail in the spring and summer.

MILES AND DIRECTIONS

0.0 Find the path that begins on the opposite side of the road from the parking area, toward the north.

0.3 Trail split: This is the start of the loop. Turn left to hike in a clockwise direction.

0.6 Trail junction; stay right.

1.1 Trail junction; you've closed the loop. Turn left and retrace your steps back to the car.

1.3 Arrive back at the car.

FUN FACTOR: WHO IS LADY BIRD?

Lady Bird Johnson was an influential woman who defined the modern-day office of the first lady. Her list of lifetime accomplishments is worthy of a book in itself, and if you're searching for inspiration of what it means to be a leader who lives a mission, her story is a great place to start. She was born Claudia Alta Taylor in 1912, but it only took a few years for her to garner the nickname Lady Bird, which became her only name (for all intents and purposes) for the balance of her life. She is famous for work to beautify America through conservation, and it was her husband who signed the 1964 Wilderness Act into law. Between the two of them, they had meaningful influence on our public lands, and because of her work, President Nixon dedicated this grove to her in 1969, "In recognition of her dedicated service to the cause of preserving and enhancing America's natural beauty for the enjoyment of all the people." The ceremony was a result of finally passing the bill to create Redwood National Park.

13 MANZANITA LAKE LOOP

Plentiful wildlife? Check. Stunning views of the volcanic Mount Lassen? Check. Swimming options galore? Double-check. The glowing sunsets are plenty for the parents, but kids also love the Manzanita Lake Loop thanks to the variety of trail options for sheer entertainment.

Start: Manzanita Lake trailhead
Distance: 2.0-mile loop
Hiking time: About 2 hours
Difficulty: Easy
Elevation gain: 45 feet
Trail surface: Dirt and pavement
Hours open: Open daily, 24 hours a day
Best season: Late spring to early autumn
Water: Fill up at the visitor center
Toilets: At the trailhead
Nursing benches: No
Stroller-friendly: Yes
Potential child hazards: None

Other trail users: None
Dogs: Not allowed
Land status: National Park Service
Nearest town: Viola
Fees and permits: Fee to enter the park, or purchase America the Beautiful annual pass
Maps: Lassen Volcanic National Park map
Trail contact: Lassen Volcanic National Park, PO Box 100, Mineral, CA 96063; (530) 595-4480; www.nps.gov/lavo
Gear suggestions: Trekking poles and sturdy shoes

FINDING THE TRAILHEAD

From Redding, take CA 44 east for approximately 47 miles. Turn right to head south on CA 89 toward the park entrance. The trailhead parking is at the visitor center just a mile down the road. The parking area has multiple spots and is constantly busy, but chances are someone is likely leaving their spot so be patient. GPS: N40 32.18' / W121 33.78'

THE HIKE

This mellow 2.0-mile saunter around Manzanita Lake can be enjoyed at any time, but we've taken it upon ourselves to create a perfect itinerary for you.

After sleeping under the stars at the nearby Manzanita Lake Campground, enjoy a leisurely family breakfast at camp before wandering down to Manzanita Lake. Here, you and the kids can while away the warmer afternoon hours by splashing in the water or paddling across the glimmering glass in a rented kayak or on a stand-up paddleboard. As the sun begins to dip below the horizon and the soaring temperatures decrease, towel off and grab some snacks for your backpack. It's time to hike.

To be fair, the Manzanita Lake Loop makes for a wonderful hike at any time of the day. But, the lake is often crowded midday with picnickers and swimmers—just like you!—looking to cool off in the sparkling water. As the day winds down, these families all return to their campsites or cabins, leaving a serene and tranquil experience for the intrepid family of hikers willing to stick around for a while.

Bonus: Sunrises and sunsets at Manzanita Lake are a sight not to be missed. Since children don't often cooperate with predawn wakeup calls, we're Team Sunset.

Taking a family cooldown after a midsummer hike

Begin your hike at the visitor center just off CA 89, the main route into the park. Head south past the museum, center, and parking area until you reach the small, paved path. This is your route. Hike for a few minutes and you'll reach a trail junction; take a right. You'll be ambling around the lake in a counterclockwise direction, and this turn is the beginning of your adventure.

After a quarter-mile, the trail will curve north–northwest and begin wrapping along the north side of Manzanita Lake. For better or worse, this section of the hike is also the noisiest thanks to its proximity to the nearby highway. However, the buzz of traffic is easily ignorable if you focus your attention on Mount Lassen looming across the water. While it's certainly not close, the towering massif feels as if you could reach out and grab its summit. Soak in these views because eventually, they will be at your back.

Continue trending northwest as the trail hugs the lake to your left. At roughly 0.6 mile, the route will turn southward as it parallels the western shoreline of Manzanita Lake. At 0.7 mile, you'll come across a small bridge that crosses over Manzanita Creek as the babbling water exits the lake and begins its journey downstream. If the kiddos are already experiencing tired legs, look for the old-fashioned bench created out of a downed tree. It is a comfortable spot to rest weary feet and admire the surrounding scenery. Pro tip: Dragonflies are aplenty in this area, so challenge your children to a game of, "Who can count more?"

After the bench, hike south along the lakeside, following its curves as it turns eastward before looping back toward the west yet again. As the trail just begins to head south again at 1.0 mile, you'll encounter a series of five steps: These are the only steps on the entire hike!

Beautiful views of Lassen Peak from across Manzanita Lake Loop

At 1.1 miles, the trail turns east as you hike along the southern shoreline of Manzanita Lake. Depending on the season, this area is a prime lookout for ducks and geese in the water. If you happen to visit in the spring, your kids may be lucky enough to spot a proud mama duck with a line of fuzzy babies waddling behind her.

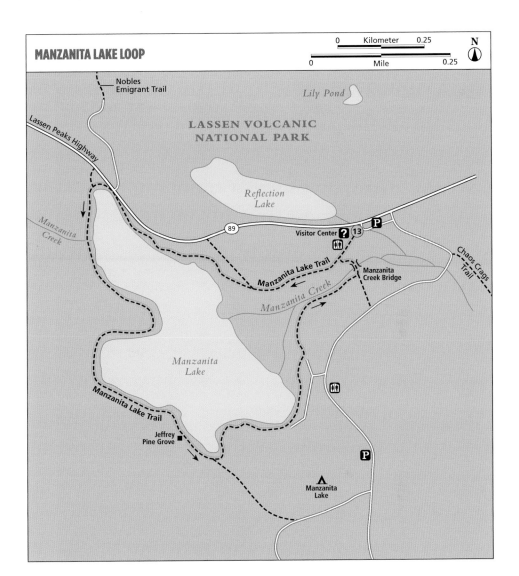

FUN FACTOR: EXPLORE THE MANZANITA LAKE CAMPGROUND

As the biggest campground in Lassen National Park, Manzanita Lake Campground is perfect for families who want to tent camp or bring a trailer or RV. Rustic camping cabins are also available for those not quite willing to sleep on the ground. Since the campground is situated smack against the lake, it is easy to entertain kids with all the activities offered. Kayaks, paddleboards, and canoes are all available to rent at the boat launch. Or, if you have a budding angler in your group, the fly-fishing is superb with the lake boasting plenty of large trout. Just be aware that fishing is limited to catch-and-release and only with a single, barbless hook. You may only use an artificial fly or lure; no living or nonliving bait allowed.

Trailside views at the halfway point

As you reach 1.3 miles and the southernmost tip of the lake, you'll also reach a trail junction with another path that trends inland. This is the route that takes hikers into the Manzanita Campground referenced in the sidebar.

As you near the end of the hike, the trail will begin curving back toward the north and views of Lassen will gradually disappear at your back. You'll pass the boat ramp at 1.5 miles and a picnic area soon thereafter. During this section, the trail feels a bit spotty so stay parallel to the parking lot as you trek through the trees. You'll quickly pick up the solid trail after this. Follow it away from the lake and over the Manzanita Creek bridge at 1.8 miles. The trail turns toward the right and you'll find yourself back at the visitor center.

MILES AND DIRECTIONS

0.0   Begin at the trailhead at the visitor center off CA 89. You'll find the good, paved path leaving from the southwest side of the lot.

0.1   Trail junction; stay right to begin the loop in a counterclockwise direction.

0.4   The trail run alongside the highway as it skirts the north side of the lake.

0.6   Follow the route as it turns south and begins heading along the west side of Manzanita Lake.

We are not above bribery to get our daughter to hike—she earned this one!

0.7   Enjoy the makeshift bench after crossing over Manzanita Creek.

1.0   Climb the five steps, the only steps on the entire hike.

1.3   Trail junction; stay left and away from the campground.

1.5   Hike by the boat launch for the lake.

1.6   Pass through the picnic area as the trail begins moving away from the lake.

1.8   Trail junction; turn left and cross the bridge over Manzanita Creek.

1.85   Trail junction; turn right and return to the parking area.

2.0   Arrive back at the trailhead.

14 RIM TRAIL

Thirty miles north of Eureka sits Sue-Meg State Park, a hidden gem chock-full of kid-friendly fun. Foggy mornings, lush singletrack, glimmering tidepools, and unbelievable wildlife spotting (both dolphins and whales) are just a few of the offerings found within this 1-square-mile park. To be sure, it's small, but Sue-Meg makes up for its tiny stature with a large number of unexplored possibilities.

Start: Rim trailhead
Distance: 1.9-mile one way
Hiking time: About 2 hours
Difficulty: Easy
Elevation gain: 180 feet
Trail surface: Dirt and rock
Hours open: Dawn to dusk
Best season: Late spring to early autumn
Water: In the campground
Toilets: At the parking lot
Nursing benches: No
Stroller-friendly: No

Potential child hazards: Steep cliffs falling into the ocean at the overlooks
Other trail users: None
Dogs: Not allowed
Land status: California Department of Parks and Recreation
Nearest town: Trinidad
Fees and permits: Day-use fee
Maps: Sue-Meg State Park brochure
Trail contact: Sue-Meg State Park, 4150 Patrick's Point Dr., Trinidad, CA 95570; (707) 667-3570; www.parks.ca.gov/?page_id=417
Gear suggestions: Sturdy shoes

FINDING THE TRAILHEAD

From Redding, take CA 299 west for approximately 135 miles. Take the exit onto US 101 north toward Crescent City and go 18 miles. Take exit 734 for Patrick's Point Drive and then follow signs for the Agate Beach Campground parking area. The trailhead technically starts just up the road, but you can only park at the campground. Alternatively, you can park at Palmer's Point overlook and hike the trail the opposite direction. GPS: N41 7.42' / W124 9.33'

THE HIKE

Sue-Meg State Park State Park doesn't naturally boast any redwood trees, so hikers often overlook this mystical place in favor of nearby Redwood National Park. That's a mistake. For starters, a thick, ethereal fog frequently shrouds the region, often blanketing the Rim Trail for days at a time. While this is less than ideal for views, it makes this trail a great option for families wanting to beat the heat more commonly found in other parts of Northern California. If you can score a rare bluebird day (more likely in the spring and fall) with twinkling sunshine and glimmering ocean waves below, you and the kids are in for a world-class treat.

The core, 2-mile main segment of the Rim Trail stretches from one end of the park to the other, beginning at Agate Beach and terminating at Palmer's Point. Families can begin at either trailhead since there is parking readily available along the whole trek. And, with barely more than 100 feet of climbing, the Rim Trail isn't more difficult in one direction. Bottom line: Flip a coin or ask your kiddos which trailhead they want to select as the beginning.

Coastal exploring with mama and daughter

The trail shifts between coastal views and forested walks.

Holding hands on top
of Wedding Rock

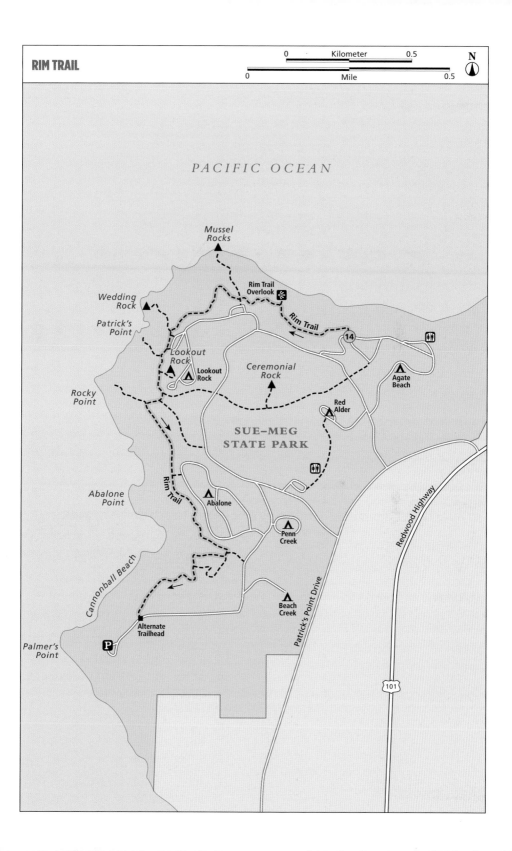

0   Kilometer   0.5

0   Mile   0.5

N

PACIFIC OCEAN

Mussel
Rocks

Rim Trail
Overlook

Rim Trail

Wedding
Rock

Patrick's
Point

Lookout
Rock

Lookout
Rock

Ceremonial
Rock

14

Agate
Beach

Rocky
Point

Red
Alder

SUE–MEG
STATE PARK

Abalone
Point

Rim Trail

Abalone

Penn
Creek

Cannonball Beach

Beach
Creek

Patrick's Point Drive

Redwood Highway

Alternate
Trailhead

P

Palmer's
Point

101

Looking south along the coast from Wedding Rock

Assuming you begin at Agate Beach, you'll almost immediately notice a stunning ocean overlook with crashing whitecaps rolling into the sand-strewn shoreline as cliffs filled with Sitka spruce rise up from within an understory of blackberry and fern plants. This is the Agate Beach Overlook, and it's giving you a small hint of the views to come.

Continue past a small spur trail at ⅛ of a mile and once again enter a thick and dense forest that practically teems with moisture on foggy days. A small stream on your left called Beaver Creek provides a constant sound machine, but the views to your right are the real showstoppers. And, once you cross over the small waterfall via a kid-approved bridge, mile 0.5 will bring you to the first of four main spur trails.

In addition to the core Rim Trail, there are four quarter-mile spur trails that direct hikers down the bluffs to the shoreline. The first descends 146 stairs down the Mussel Rocks Trail where a lovely viewpoint provides fishing opportunities galore. ***Note:*** These spur trails are not included in the overall mileage and elevation statistics.

The Rim Trail itself continues on, climbing a few stairs before turning south and passing between two large boulders. From there, you'll see the first picnic area of the journey and a great spot for little legs to rest.

The ocean views abound as the trail continues west, passing a second picnic spot (with water). Not long after, you'll come across a trail split; stay right to avoid the busy parking area for Wedding Rock. You'll then encounter the second trail spur that once again descends a steep staircase before ascending the 120-foot-tall sea stack known as Wedding Rock. This is a quite popular destination for families, and children love playing on the rocks—just keep an eye on the youngest kiddos. Pro tip: Wedding Rock is a great location for whale watching!

Hike south along the Rim Trail until you come across the paved, wheelchair-accessible path. Just afterwards, you'll find the third spur trail, marked simply as the Overlook Trail. This route hikes down toward an overlook that offers a postcard-worthy view of the very same Wedding Rock that you just scampered around.

From there, the Rim Trail circumnavigates the base of Lookout Rock (on the left) before arriving at the final spur trail on the right, Rocky Point Trail. If you opt to tackle this final spur, it's roughly ⅛ of a mile to the top of the sea stack and back.

Enjoy a mellow descent through the Sitka spruce forest before climbing back up and heading into an open alder forest that offers frequent ocean views between the trees. Continue through the forest until you're skirting the western edge of the Abalone Campground. At roughly 1⅛ mile, you'll notice a small side trail that takes you to Abalone Point, the area where the Indigenous Yurok once had a seasonal village (see sidebar).

Eventually you'll meet another paved trail that's leaving Abalone Campground before crossing another bridge and arriving at a three-way trail split: the left returns to the original trailhead via a longer loop, the middle goes to the Campfire Center, and the right descends down to Palmer's Point. For this guide, we're headed to Palmer's Point.

Follow Penn Creek to another bench and an overlook before ambling through a sea of pine and spruce trees. The trail itself ends just before 1.75 miles, but continue down the shoulder of the paved road until you arrive at the picnic area and the final spur trail to the end of Palmer's Point.

MILES AND DIRECTIONS

0.0   Begin at the Agate Beach Trailhead and find the trail on the west side of the parking area.

0.1   Intersection with your first spur trail but stay on the main trail. On the right, admire the view of Mussel Rocks to the northwest and Agate Beach to the northeast.

0.35   Cross a bridge just above a small waterfall.

0.5   Trail junction; spur to Mussels Rocks heads out to the right.

0.6   Trail junction; spur to Wedding Rock on the right.

0.75   Trail junction; the Patrick's Point spur trail heads to the right.

1.1   Trail junction; spur trail to Abalone Point descends to the right.

1.4   Intersection with the paved path from Abalone Campground; turn right.

1.5   Cross bridge over Beach Creek.

1.7   Trail ends and transitions to the paved road to Palmer's Point.

1.9   Arrive at the end of the paved road and the picnic area. You've reached the end.

15 STONEY CREEK SWIM AREA TRAIL

Ditch the neighborhood pool in favor of this natural swim area that comes with a (small) side of hiking. The Stoney Creek Swim Area Trail doesn't require much effort, which makes it a solid choice for little legs, hot days, and unadulterated family time.

Start: Stoney Creek Swim Area parking lot
Distance: 0.3 mile to 0.6 mile one way
Hiking time: 30 minutes to 1 hour
Difficulty: Easy
Elevation gain: 20 to 40 feet
Trail surface: Dirt, rock, and sand
Hours open: Dawn to dusk
Best season: Late spring to late summer
Water: At the parking lot
Toilets: At the parking lot
Nursing benches: Tables in the picnic area
Stroller-friendly: Paved path to the beach but nowhere else

Potential child hazards: Supervision needed in and around the lake
Other trail users: None
Dogs: Not allowed
Land status: US Forest Service
Nearest town: Weaverville
Fees and permits: Day-use fee
Maps: Shasta-Trinity National Forest, Stoney Creek Swim Area map
Trail contact: Weaverville Ranger Station, PO Box 1190, Weaverville, CA 96093; (530) 623-2121; www.fs .usda.gov/stnf
Gear suggestions: Sturdy shoes and sand toys

FINDING THE TRAILHEAD

From Redding, take CA 299 west for approximately 28 miles. Turn right onto Trinity Dam Boulevard for 4.6 miles before turning left on Lewiston Turnpike Road. After 0.7 miles, take another slight left onto Rush Creek Road (toward CA 3 north) and continue for approximately 8.4 miles. Merge onto CA 3 north for 7 miles. The parking lot for Stoney Creek Swim Area will be on your left. Parking is limited and can be very busy on summer weekends. GPS: N40 51.06' / W122 51.11'

THE HIKE

Nestled on the banks of Stoney Creek sits this picturesque little swim area that appeals to kids, both young and old. In reality, this hike is less trail and more water, but we feel that ratio often hits the sweet spot on toasty-hot summer afternoons.

The swimming hole sits on the Stuart Fork Arm of Trinity Lake, one of the largest artificial lakes (reservoirs) in California. Thanks to a smaller dam on Stoney Creek, a sizable pool of water gathers just north of CA 3 and creates a refreshing swimming hole. The sandy beach on the west side of the pool has a sloping hillside so it resembles a zero-depth entry, making it possible for young children to enjoy ankle-deep water too. The shallow end doesn't last long—maybe 4 or 5 feet—before it plunges into deeper water that requires swimming abilities. But there is plenty of beach fun to go around, in large thanks to the nearby picnic tables and grills.

Parent-approved rock jumping in the wading area

Trekking upriver from the main wading area

Creekside exploring beside the trail

From the parking area, it's easy to see your destination below. Begin on the paved path on the north side of the parking lot. Within a few steps, you'll pass a building on your left. These are the restrooms and changing areas for parents with sandy diapers.

Continue hiking the paved path as it switchbacks down the hillside. You'll see two spur trails with stairs that cut directly downhill; all of the routes funnel to the same spot, so choose one that best suits your abilities.

Summertime bloom above the creek at the far end of the trail

FUN FACTOR: VISIT THE SCOTT MUSEUM

North Trinity Lake and the surrounding areas may be sleepy, but the area is rife with history. One such example is the Scott Museum in Trinity Center, a 20-minute drive from the Stoney Creek Swimming Area. Established by the Scott family, this tiny museum emphasizes the mining, timber, and ranching activities that define the region. When the museum is open, docents are on-site to educate families about the collection of antiques inside the museum. Hours: June 1–Sept 1, Tues through Sat, noon to 4 p.m. Cost: Donation.

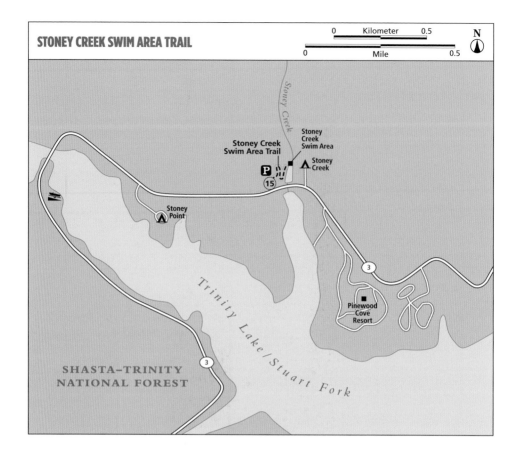

Once you've reached the sandy beach, you can make a choice. Most families grab a patch of sand and dive into the swimming hole, enjoying the large pool where it is the deepest and most enjoyable. However, the main beach area is also the most crowded. If you're hoping for a little more quiet time, turn left and head north to follow alongside Stoney Creek. While you won't find any established picnic areas or large swimming holes, there are a few small patches of dirt streamside where you can throw down a towel and splash in the sparkling (and shallow) water, free from the crowds a short walk behind you.

MILES AND DIRECTIONS

0.0   Begin hiking on the paved path leaving from the northeast corner of the circular parking area.

0.05   Pass by the restrooms and changing rooms on the left side.

0.1   Turn sharply to the right as the path switchbacks down the hillside.

0.15   Reach the largest swimming pool of the Stoney Creek Swim Area. Explore up and down the water for a good spot for your towels. Whenever you're done splashing, turn around and retrace your steps back to the car.

16 STOUT MEMORIAL GROVE TRAIL

The National Park Service refers to the Stout Grove of redwoods as the "beating heart" of Jedediah Smith Redwoods State Park, and these centuries-old trees deserve the moniker. The hike itself is mellow and easy—worthy of the littles' legs—which is a good thing since getting to the trail takes some serious effort.

Start: Stout Memorial Grove trailhead
Distance: 0.6-mile loop
Hiking time: About 1 hour
Difficulty: Easy
Elevation gain: 30 feet
Trail surface: Dirt
Hours open: Sunrise to sunset
Best season: Any season
Water: At the campground visitor center
Toilets: At the campground visitor center
Nursing benches: At Jedediah Smith Campground Picnic Area
Stroller-friendly: Yes

Potential child hazards: Poison oak along the trail edges and abundant amount of ticks
Other trail users: None
Dogs: Not allowed
Land status: California Department of Parks and Recreation
Nearest town: Crescent City
Fees and permits: Fee
Maps: Jedediah Smith Redwoods State Park brochure
Trail contact: Jedediah Smith Redwoods State Park, 1111 Second St., Crescent City, CA 95531; (707) 464-6101; https://www.parks.ca.gov/?page_id=413
Gear suggestions: Sturdy shoes

FINDING THE TRAILHEAD

From Eureka, take US 101 north for approximately 85 miles. Take exit 794 toward Grants Pass and continue on US 199 north for approximately 7 miles. Take a right immediately after the sign for river access to Myrtle Beach onto South Fork Road. After 0.5 mile, turn right onto Douglas Park Drive for 1.3 miles and then continue onto Howland Hill Road for another mile. The road to the trailhead is on your right. Parking is limited. GPS: N41 47.38 / W124 5.09'

THE HIKE

The Stout Memorial Grove was preserved in 1929 when Clara Stout donated the 44-acre grove to the Save-the-Redwoods League in honor of her late husband. Today, we're grateful that she did so, because the Stout Grove is easily one of the best-kept gems in Northern California.

Not only are the redwoods arguably the most beautiful coastal redwoods in the entirety of Jedediah Smith Redwoods State Park, but the Stout Grove is also unique: Only coastal redwoods grow in the grove. You cannot spot a single other type of tree, aside from the lush understory of the ferns so prevalent in the region. This means the sunlight trickles down from high up in the canopy of the redwoods and creates a dazzling effect as it fills the air surrounding the tree trunks.

Of course, nothing worthwhile is ever easy, and this hike is representative of that belief. While the hike itself is merely a half-mile journey, getting to the grove takes some work.

Pictures don't do this grove justice—it can rearrange your personal perspective of your place in the universe.

There are two ways to approach this hike. First, you can drive the 6 miles up the eastern section of Howland Hill Road. This approach is open year-round, but the road is not paved and is very windy and bumpy. Small passenger cars can make it work, but larger vehicles, trailers, and RVs cannot. (Plus, there is no parking for RVs and trailers at the trailhead.)

For the eastern section option, park your vehicle at the Jedediah Smith Redwoods State Park Campground Day Use Area. There is a fee, but all vehicles are welcome, including the larger variety. From the campground, walk toward the Smith River where you'll find a hiking trail winding upstream. This riverside route is about a half-mile long and traverses the hiking bridge that dumps visitors into Stout Grove. Caveat: Not only does this add on extra mileage, but this approach is only open in the summer.

Regardless of which way you tackle the grove, you're in for a treat. We began the hike at the trailhead off Howland Hill Road and completed the loop in a clockwise direction.

Immediately, it's noticeable how little sunlight reaches the forest floor where the fern and redwood sorrel (the green, clover-like groundcover) snatch up every tidbit of light.

Because there are no other trees in the grove, each trunk feels spacious and widely spread from the next. It's also easy to appreciate their vastness since the canopy isn't cluttered with other, shorter trees. As you look into the sky, you'll see each individual treetop silhouetted against the clouds. It's almost as if the redwood is acting as a sentry and keeping a watch out in order to protect her grove.

If your neck needs a break, consider looking at the ground instead. When you do, you may spot a few yellow blobs dotting the base of the trees. These are banana slugs, the ubiquitous mascot at the University of California–Santa Cruz. These mollusks are

Continuing on the trail as it wraps through the grove

commonly found on the forest floor of the redwoods, and kids love looking at the shell-less creatures.

While walking the loop, you'll encounter two different trail junctions. The first provides access to the summer footbridge and trail that eventually leads to the Jedediah Smith campground and secondary parking area. The second is the River Trail, a path that travels east and then parallel to the Smith River before ending at Little Bald Hills Trailhead.

FUN FACTOR: CAMP UNDER OLD-GROWTH REDWOODS

Jedediah Smith Campground is the only campground in all of Redwood National and State Parks that has lowland redwood trees right there in the campsites. It's a drive-in campground, so no backpacking or hiking is needed. However, it is best suited for tents rather than trailers or RVs. Trailers that are less than 21 feet and RVs up to 25 feet are technically allowed, but there aren't any hookups. And, as we mentioned earlier in the chapter, the approach road is windy, small, and bumpy, which can be challenging in a larger vehicle.

All that said, Jed Smith Campground is a truly special place to spend a night or two, and kids absolutely love running laps beneath the shady protection of the redwoods. Pro tip: Some of the sites can be noisy, especially those that are near the highway. Sites 47–58 are the quietest and actually sit beneath redwoods, but they get snapped up quickly. Plan your trip well in advance!

The open spaces in the grove give a good sense of scale and grandeur.

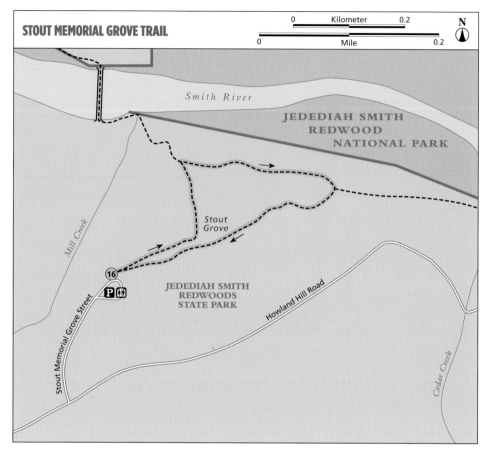

While you're out there, keep an eye out for the Stout Tree. As the tallest tree in the grove, the Stout Tree is 16 feet in diameter and 340 feet tall!

MILES AND DIRECTIONS

0.0 Begin hiking at the trailhead off Howland Hill Road. Find the trail that leaves from the north side of the parking lot.

0.05 Almost immediately, the trail splits. Stay left.

0.1 Trail junction: stay left to begin the loop in a clockwise direction.

0.2 Trail junction: stay right.

0.3 Trail junction: stay right.

0.55 Merge back onto the main trail.

0.6 Return to the parking lot.

17 SUBWAY CAVE LAVA TUBE

Hidden just outside of Lassen National Park, the Subway Cave Lava Tube is easy to miss since it doesn't receive national park fanfare. Trust us: This underground and otherworldly experience is one that kids love. After all, what's more stimulating than exploring a dark and damp lava cave?

Start: Subway Cave trailhead
Distance: 0.7-mile loop
Hiking time: About 30 minutes
Difficulty: Easy
Elevation gain: 20 feet (to descend into the cave via a stone staircase)
Trail surface: Dirt and rock
Hours open: Dawn to dusk (closed in the winter months)
Best season: Late spring to early autumn
Water: At the campground across the road
Toilets: At the trailhead
Nursing benches: No
Stroller-friendly: No

Potential child hazards: Bats are known to inhabit the cave.
Other trail users: None
Dogs: Not allowed
Land status: US Forest Service
Nearest town: Old Station
Fees and permits: No, but donations are welcome.
Maps: USFS Lassen National Forest, Hat Creek Recreation Map, and Subway Cave trail map
Trail contact: Hat Creek Ranger District, 43225 E. Hwy. 299, Fall River Mills, CA 96028; (530) 336-5521; www.fs.usda.gov/recarea/lassen
Gear suggestions: Sturdy shoes and a flashlight

FINDING THE TRAILHEAD

From Redding, take CA 44 east for approximately 60 miles. Just after Old Station, stay straight onto CA 89 north for 0.3 mile. The road to the parking area will be on your right across from Cave Campground. There is usually plenty of parking, but RVs and trailers might have a tough time turning around. GPS: N40 41.16′ / W121 25.14′

THE HIKE

Lassen National Park is rife with volcanic history, but the boundary line doesn't mean the good stuff stops once you exit the park. The Subway Cave Lava Tube is one such example, boasting an almost-ethereal lava cave that stretches for more than a third of a mile, entertaining kiddos with aptly-named segments like the Devil's Doorway, Stubtoe Hall, and Lucifer's Cul-de-sac.

Start by impressing your children with a little hip knowledge. Less than 20,000 years ago, a series of fissures (cracks in the earth) released a bunch of lava from the Hat Creek flow. In fact, so much lava pooled through the region that it even reached Hat Creek Valley, more than 16 miles to the north.

But, thanks to the chillier elements found aboveground, the top of the lava crust eventually cooled off and hardened, ultimately creating an unbreakable top surface. This crust also insulated the still-flowing lava found beneath, and the molten rivers continued to flow like earthworms moving through soil. When the lava eventually drained away, tube-like caves were left behind. Subway Cave is one such tube, and we only have access to it thanks to a top crust (or roof) that collapsed many years ago.

Follow the dirt trail as it heads toward the opening in the earth.

Looking down into the maw

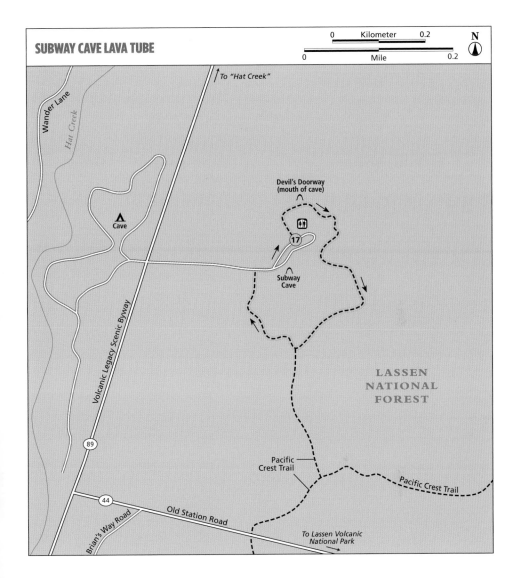

0   Kilometer   0.2

0   Mile   0.2

N

To "Hat Creek"

Wander Lane

Hat Creek

Cave

Devil's Doorway
(mouth of cave)

17

Subway
Cave

Volcanic Legacy Scenic Byway

LASSEN
NATIONAL
FOREST

89

Pacific
Crest Trail

Pacific Crest Trail

44

Brian's Way Road

Old Station Road

To Lassen Volcanic
National Park

Who said dad knowledge isn't cool?

It's important to explain this to younger children before visiting the cave, because the entrance may appear daunting otherwise. After parking in the lot, you'll walk for roughly 5 minutes before reaching the beginning of the cave, aptly named the Devil's Doorway. A staircase with a metal rail descends into darkness with the path disappearing beyond the 20-foot-wide gaping opening. The scant bit of light creeping into the cave from the staircase is your last chance to actually see the rough and jagged terrain on the floor, so take a good look. Pro tip: Don't forget a flashlight or headlamp. You definitely need one for this cave!

Continue walking through a widened section known as Stubtoe Hall, comically referencing the number of folks who slam their toes on the uneven ground. Just after Stubtoe, the trail narrows and continues to darken. Hike through this tight section for less than a

Once inside, the temperature drops significantly, making it a nice respite on summer days.

Looking into the tube—don't forget a headlamp!

tenth of a mile before you reach what appears to be a trail split. You've reached Lucifer's Cul-de-sac.

Take a moment to wander to the left and into the cul-de-sac. You'll quickly realize that it wasn't a trail split; this is just a large side cavern with upwards of 15-foot-tall ceilings. It's impressive, but the biggest chamber is yet to come.

Head back to the main route and stay to the right. In just a few minutes, you'll reach the largest of the chambers, referred to as The Sanctum. Since The Sanctum is so big (relative to the tube), it doesn't feel as if it is a "side room" in the same way that Lucifer's Cul-de-sac does. If you don't pay attention, you may wander through the large space thinking it's just a bigger portion of the tube itself.

Once you've explored The Sanctum, you're almost through the Subway Cave. The tube grows narrow once more and funnels hikers through a section known as Lavacicle Lane. (Think: lava + icicle.) This name comes from the fun lava stalactites hanging from the ceiling in this portion of the hike, and it's definitely worth spending extra time in here with your flashlight.

After Lavacicle Lane, you'll notice portions of daylight filtering through the cave. You're nearing the end. Just before you reach the exit staircase, you'll hike through yet another collapse known as Rattlesnake Collapse. It was this cave-in that created the exit path you're about to use.

Climb up the stairs into the daylight. From here, take a sharp right and follow the aboveground path back to the parking lot.

MILES AND DIRECTIONS

0.0 Begin at the Subway Cave Trailhead on the trail that leaves from the north side of the parking area.

0.1 Reach the metal staircase and descend through the entrance known as Devil's Doorway.

0.3 Begin to notice daylight again as your reach Rattlesnake Collapse near the exit stairway. Climb the stairs, turn right, and follow the path back toward the trailhead.

0.7 You've reached the parking lot.

18 TRINITY LAKESHORE TRAIL

This easy trail connects multiple camping areas along the north side of Stuart Fork Arm of Trinity Lake. Since it's not a loop, we recommend setting up a car shuttle from one end to the other (unless you're trying to prove a point to your kids about finding fun no matter where they are). If you only have one vehicle, we recommend pairing this with the Stoney Creek hike. Drop a responsible adult and your kids off at Stoney Creek, drive your car down to the Clark Springs campground, and then either hitchhike or walk your way back to Stoney Creek.

Start: Stoney Creek Swim Area parking lot
Distance: 8.5-mile out-and-back
Hiking time: About 6 hours
Difficulty: Moderate
Elevation gain: 520 feet
Trail surface: Dirt
Hours open: Dawn to dusk
Best season: Late spring to early autumn
Water: At the Stoney Creek Swim Area parking lot
Toilets: At the Stoney Creek Swim Area parking lot
Nursing benches: None

Stroller-friendly: No
Potential child hazards: None
Other trail users: None
Dogs: Allowed on leash
Land status: US Forest Service
Nearest town: Weaverville
Fees and permits: None
Maps: Shasta-Trinity National Forest, Trinity Lakeshore map
Trail contact: Weaverville Ranger Station, PO Box 1190, Weaverville, CA 96093; (530) 623-2121; www.fs.usda.gov/stnf
Gear suggestions: Sturdy shoes

FINDING THE TRAILHEAD

From Redding, take CA 299 west for approximately 28 miles. Turn right onto Trinity Dam Boulevard for 4.6 miles before turning left on Lewiston Turnpike Road. After 0.7 miles, take another slight left onto Rush Creek Road (toward CA 3 north) and continue for approximately 8.4 miles. Merge onto CA 3 north and go 10 miles. Turn right onto Rainier Road and park at the Clark Springs Campground parking lot. The trail starts at the southwestern end of the parking lot. GPS: N40 51.50' / W122 48.81'

THE HIKE

Our favorite way to do this is by combining it with an overnight stay in one of the campgrounds at either end of the hike. This area is unusually quiet—even by California standards—and when we've visited here in the height of summer, we've had no trouble finding a campground. Most are in nicely wooded areas with plenty of shade, but also a really quick walk to the edge of the lake. We'd highly recommend this area as a simple way to ease into camping, and if your kid(s) lose their minds in the middle of the night, it's relatively likely you won't have too many neighbors to worry about.

If you don't take the camping option, park at the large turnout near the exit to Pinewood Cove, which is just across the highway from the Stoney Creek area. Follow the path south until you approach the lakeshore at the far side of Pinewood Cove, and you'll

Looking out across the Stuart Arm

TRINITY LAKESHORE
TRAIL

LENGTH - 4 MI.
TRAIL GRADE - 2-25%
CROSS SLOPE - 3%
TRAIL WIDTH - 18"

The start of the trail on the western end

This trail also offers good opportunities to talk about water conservation.

Much of the trail runs on the edge of the forest with both shade and views.

see a wooden sign that marks the start of the singletrack trail as it heads east. From here you have commanding views of the Stuart Fork Arm of Trinity Lake for almost the entire duration of the hike, as the trail skirts the edge of the trees for the duration.

Trinity Lake exists because of the Trinity Dam, which started construction in 1961. By the time the dam filled 2 years later, it had become the third-largest lake in California with 145 miles of shoreline; an aerial view shows the multiple arms that splay out from

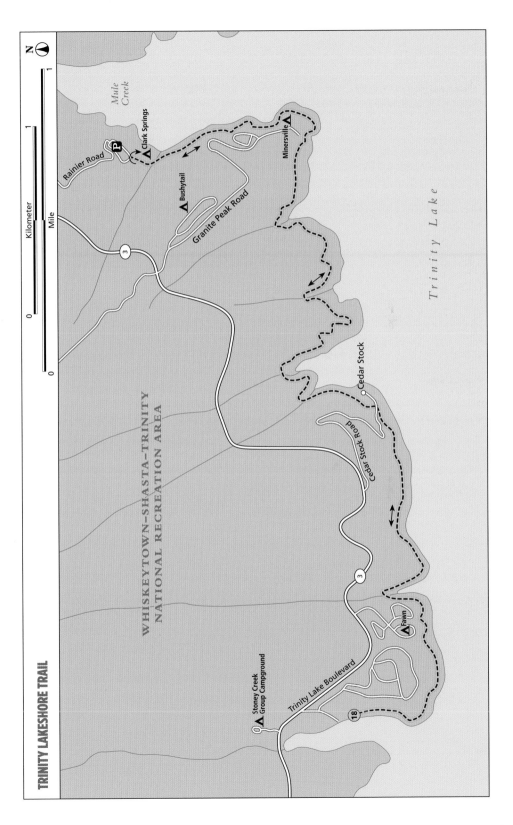

TRINITY LAKESHORE TRAIL

Rainier Road

P

Clark Springs

Mule Creek

Bushytail

Granite Peak Road

Minersville

WHISKEYTOWN–SHASTA–TRINITY
NATIONAL RECREATION AREA

Trinity Lake

Cedar Stock

Cedar Stock Road

Stoney Creek Group Campground

Fawn

Trinity Lake Boulevard

N

Kilometer

Mile

0   1

3

18

FUN FACTOR: SLEEP ON A BOAT

If you really want to splurge and try a different type of camping, Trinity Lake is a perfect chance to try your hand at houseboating. We've personally loved all of the houseboating trips we've done as a family, as the conveniences of a fully functioning kitchen and bathroom can be a real luxury when you've had a boat-full of kids playing outside all day. The Trinity Lake Resort & Marina is right in the middle of this hike, and there are few things that will thrill your offspring as much as having a floating house with a slide permanently attached to it.

the center, which make for glassy waterskiing in the morning hours. This particular hike only shows a small portion of the lake, as its total length of 19 miles mostly extends north from the Stuart Arm. One other piece of trivia: the lake was temporarily renamed Clair Engle Lake in 1964, but 33 years later the name still had not really taken with the locals, and it officially returned to its original title of Trinity Lake.

As you continue east along the trail, you'll consistently undulate up and down as you track the shoreline. Considering there's only about 250 feet of gain for each direction of the route, it's never enough to be outright exhausting, but little legs may get tired after a couple miles of hiking. The terrain and scenery generally stays the same, punctuated by shifting views of the lake and waving at folks at campsites. If 4 miles feels a bit too ambitious for your crew, you can simply turn around after a mile or two of hiking and head back to the trailhead. This is one of those hikes where you can let your kids stop, meander, and allow their imaginations run wild even if their hiking pace does not, as you're not going to miss some incredible destination experience if you don't make it to the end.

MILES AND DIRECTIONS

0.0 From the parking area at Stoney Creek, hop across the highway and follow the paved road that also acts as the entrance to Pinewood Cove Resort. Follow it down toward the water where you'll see a small brown sign on the left that indicates the Trinity Lakeshore Trail.

0.2 The trail turns eastward as it wraps around the lake.

0.8 Turn sharply right as you head south along the eastern side of an inlet.

1.1 Cross over a small stream.

1.6 Pass over a road toward the Cedar Stock Marina and continue heading straight.

1.9 Cross yet another small stream.

3.6 Cross over another road that leads to the Minersville Public Boat Ramp.

3.8 Pass the Minersville Campground on the left.

4.25 Arrive at the Clark Springs Campground. Grab your car shuttle back to the Stoney Creek Swim Area or turn around and retrace your steps.

8.5 If completing the hike on foot, arrive back at the parking area.

SOUTHERN

Trailside wildflowers

19 20 LAKES BASIN: STEELHEAD LAKE

We'd already be excited about a sub-5-mile hike to one of the most stunning collections of alpine lakes in the Sierra Range, but when you add in the option for a boat ferry to cut a few miles off the trip, this one quickly jumps to the top of the bucket list. Taking the boat bump to 20 Lakes Basin drops you at the entry to the basin, and even if you only hike another mile total, it will have been worth the trip. Because of that bump, it's also a great way to test your overnight skills with your kids in a place that feels remote—without the big distances and heavy packs.

Start: Saddlebag Lake trailhead
Distance: 6.7-mile out-and-back
Hiking time: About 6 hours
Difficulty: Moderate
Elevation gain: 692 feet
Trail surface: Dirt and rock
Hours open: Dawn until dusk
Best season: Spring to autumn (road to the trailhead closes in the winter)
Water: Treated from creeks and lakes
Toilets: At the campground
Nursing benches: None
Stroller-friendly: No

Potential child hazards: None
Other trail users: None
Dogs: Allowed on leash
Land status: US Forest Service
Nearest town: Lee Vining
Fees and permits: None
Maps: Inyo National Forest, Hoover and Hall area map
Trail contact: Inyo National Forest, 351 Pacu Ln., Ste. 200, Bishop, CA 93514; (760) 873-2400; www.fs.usda .gov/inyo
Gear suggestions: Sturdy shoes and sunscreen (there is little to no shade)

FINDING THE TRAILHEAD

From Modesto, take CA 120 east for approximately 121 miles. Turn left onto Saddlebag Lake Road and go 2.5 miles. Parking is limited at Saddlebag Lake Resort. GPS: N37 57.96' / W119 16.26'

THE HIKE

Park at the Saddlebag Lake Trailhead, and should you choose the human-powered version of hiking to the far end of Saddlebag Lake, we recommend starting with the west side of the loop as it's a little bit shorter (you can decide on the way back if you want to make a loop or not). Begin by crossing the dam at the base of Saddlebag Lake, and then continue on the well-trammeled route across the loose rock fields. The footing here is a bit dodgy, so take your time, particularly if you're toting a kid carrier. After about 1.8 miles you'll come to the far end, and with all due respect to Saddlebag Lake, it will look moderately homely in hindsight once you get a first glimpse of 20 Lakes Basin. The inviting meadow, the towering granite walls, the sparkling lakes; it's like living in the best version of a Sierra daydream that never quits.

Your first lake after Saddlebag is Greenstone, which appears in front of you just as you come around the corner. Bear to the left side of the lake; there can be a series of social trails from folks coming off the boat, and if you find yourself heading north too quickly

Looking across Greenstone Lake
at the start of the day

you are likely on the wrong trail. Follow the trail as it wraps around the southeast side of Greenstone, then continue north once you hit the junction on the far side (continuing east is a great hike to Conness Lakes, but definitely more challenging). You'll pass another small junction on the far north side of Greenstone; just keep bearing north/northwest and you'll be headed toward Steelhead.

After another half-mile on the trail, you'll have a small series of ponds to your left, including Wasco Lake, and incredible views of the towering basin walls all around with North Peak directly to the west. At about 0.6 mile you'll pass another junction. Stay left to continue up toward Steelhead Lake. The trail doglegs right through the open meadows, and soon you arrive at the base of Steelhead, with a collection of other small alpine ponds to the west.

As you probably surmised from the name 20 Lakes Basin, there's plenty of good fishing up here. The brookies will generally take a moderately well-cast fly, and although the fish are not massive, you get some beautiful coloring in typically straightforward fishing conditions (barring aggressive winds, of course). Given the short hike, particularly with the ferry bump, expect to have a good amount of time up here

This is also a low-risk way to try overnight backpacking with your kids. One of our local friends brings her 4-year-old daughter up here routinely, and if you're feeling up to it, you can complete the entire 20 Lakes Basin Loop (about 8 miles altogether). Follow the same route described above, but instead of stopping at Steelhead Lake, continue to loop in a clockwise direction as you pass Shamrock Lake and curve around the back of Lake Helen. From here head south to Lundy Pass, and you'll eventually reconnect back to the north side of Saddlebag. Keep in mind this route is more challenging than Steelhead because the trail is much farther around Lake Helen.

Morning reflections of North Peak

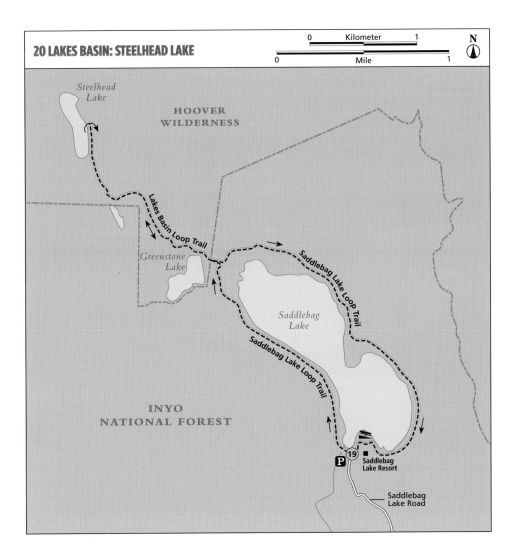

0 Kilometer 1

0 Mile 1

N

Steelhead
Lake

HOOVER
WILDERNESS

Lakes Basin Loop Trail

Greenstone
Lake

Saddlebag Lake Loop Trail

Saddlebag
Lake

Saddlebag Lake Loop Trail

INYO
NATIONAL FOREST

P 19 ■ Saddlebag
Lake Resort

Saddlebag
Lake Road

FUN FACTOR: FIND YOUR OWN ADVENTURE

If you have aspiring wayfinders, this area is perfect for choosing your own adventure and learning how to apply maps to real weekend overnight trips. Start by considering somewhere near Greenstone Lake as your basecamp (please only camp in previously impacted spots!). Then, fan out from there with lighter day packs for your daily adventures. Before your trip, sit down with a topo map and your family, and plan where you want to go explore. The Lake Conness area is a wonderful sideshow, and if you have advanced cross-country skills, your family could consider the moderately difficult scramble up to North Peak. But even if it's just milling about the basin itself, the large number of named lakes, peaks, and general clear views are perfect for testing navigation.

Carpets of Indian paintbrush thrive trailside at the far end of Saddlebag Lake.

Beautiful meadow-skipping on the way to Steelhead Lake

MILES AND DIRECTIONS

0.0	Begin in a clockwise direction at Saddlebag Lake Loop trailhead (aka go left).
1.2	Keep right at the fork to stay on Saddlebag Lake Loop trail.
1.4	Keep right to stay on Saddlebag Lake Loop trail (do not take the spur trail to your left).
1.5	Take a left onto Lakes Basin Loop trail.
2.4	Keep right at the fork to stay on Lakes Basin Loop trail.
2.6	Stay straight to keep on Lakes Basin Loop trail.
2.8	Arrive at Steelhead Lake and return back down the trail.
3.4	Stay left at the fork to continue on Lakes Basin Loop trail.
4.1	Stay left at the fork to continue the clockwise direction around Saddlebag Lake.
4.3	Take a left onto Saddlebag Lake Loop trail.
6.7	End at Saddlebag Lake trailhead.

20 BARTHOLOMEW MEMORIAL PARK TRAIL

Chalk this hike up as an "only in wine country" type of adventure. Rolling hills lead to decent elevation gain and panoramic views of historic wineries spread throughout the Sonoma Valley. On a good weather day, you can even catch a glimpse of the picturesque Golden Gate Bridge off in the distance. This trail gets your heart pumping, but pair it with a picnic for the kids and a bottle of wine from either Bartholomew Park Winery or Buena Vista Winery. Both have tasting rooms on-site, so you can enjoy the fruits of the landscape you just hiked through.

Start: Grape Stomp trailhead
Distance: 2.4-mile loop
Hiking time: About 1.5 hours
Difficulty: Easy
Elevation gain: 505 feet
Trail surface: Dirt
Hours open: 10 a.m. to 4:30 p.m.
Best season: Any season
Water: At the South Gate parking area
Toilets: At the South Gate parking area
Nursing benches: Picnic tables at the winery and a bench along the Grape Stomp Trail

Stroller-friendly: No
Potential child hazards: Several stream crossings
Other trail users: None
Dogs: Allowed on leash
Land status: Private park
Nearest town: Sonoma
Fees and permits: None
Maps: Bartholomew Park Trail map
Trail contact: Frank H. Bartholomew Foundation, 1695 Castle Rd., Sonoma, CA 95476; (707) 938-2244; www.bartholomewpark.org
Gear suggestions: Sturdy shoes

FINDING THE TRAILHEAD

From San Francisco, take US 101 north for approximately 22 miles. Take exit 460A to CA 37 toward Napa/Vallejo and go 7 miles. Turn left onto CA 121 north and go 8 miles, then turn left onto 8th Street E. Stay on 8th Street E for 3 miles until a T-stop and turn left. Then turn immediately right onto 7th Street E and go 0.3 mile. Turn right onto Castle Road and park at the Villa Parking lot (North Gate parking area). The winery parking area is only for winery guests, not hikers. You can get to the Grape Stomp trailhead by walking north through the vineyard. You can also take the paved path south to the You-Walk Miwok trailhead which has bathrooms and water. GPS: N38 17.99' / W122 25.40'

THE HIKE

It's tough to even consider this hike without first considering the history of the area. Before you set foot to trail, the first building you'll see is the reconstruction of the Haraszthy Villa (also called the Palladian Villa), overlooking the original vineyards. The entire area once was owned by a Hungarian count named Agoston Haraszthy who first planted the grapes in 1861. Then, the Buena Vista Winery followed in order to process the fruit. The villa was constructed soon thereafter.

Top: Any trail through a winery is good in our book.
Bottom left: Detail of the grapes beside the trail
Bottom right: The trail is well maintained and skips between sun and shade.

Looking back toward the winery from one of the overlooks

Unfortunately, the grapes weren't long for this world. Less than 10 years later, a disease called phylloxera (known as the silent and deadly killer since there is no cure) wiped out all of the grapevines. Haraszthy abandoned the area and the villa burned down.

The property sat in a state of disrepair until 1943 when Frank Bartholomew and his wife, Toni, purchased it. They fixed it up and eventually sold the winery. After Frank died, Toni created the memorial park and built the reconstructed villa in honor of her late husband. Today, that's where you'll find the Bartholomew Park Winery's tasting room (to enjoy after your hike!).

FUN FACTOR: BUENA VISTA WINERY IS GREAT FOR KIDS TOO

Taking kids to wine tastings is a controversial topic in the wine world, but Buena Vista Winery is easily one of the most kid-friendly wineries out there. Not only is the tour led by a historian/actor dressed up in a period costume, but the Historic Wine Tool Museum on-site has a light-and-sound show that entertains the fussiest of kids. Bonus: There is also a hedge maze where the kids can literally run wild.

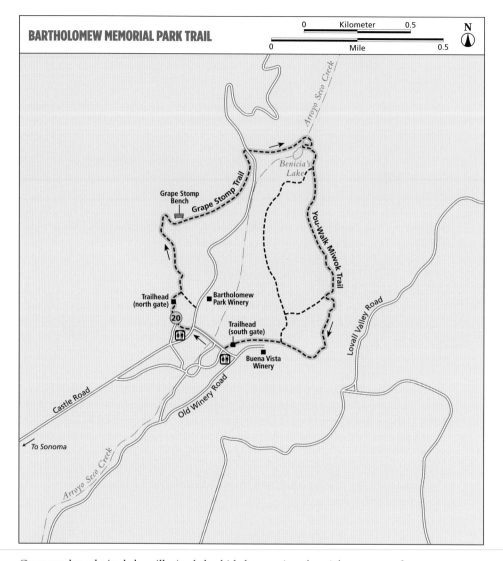

Once you've admired the villa (and the kids have enjoyed a pickup game of soccer on the lawn in front, as our daughter did), consider the hiking loop. You can tackle the loop in either direction, but for the sake of our guide, we'll share the details in a clockwise fashion. The loop itself is comprised of two trails: the Grape Stomp Trail on the western half and the You-Walk-Miwok Trail on the eastern half.

From the north end of the parking area, follow the trail for just a minute until you reach the Duck Pond on your left. From there the trail curves toward the right and reaches a gate. Head through the gate and you'll begin to leave the flat and mellow winery grounds behind you. Now, you're hiking into the rough-and-tumble backcountry.

Pass through a stream and you'll continue hiking in a dense forest filled with oak and manzanitas. This section of the hike is on the Grape Stomp Trail, and it steadily climbs up the hill while running parallel to the stream. In steeper sections, staircases are built into the hillside to make the ascent a bit more manageable (and less slippery).

Continue climbing and you'll soon arrive at the Grape Stomp bench. Take a minute to relax here and admire the views of Sonoma and San Pablo Bay—they're worth it!

Near the end of the Grape Stomp Trail, you'll pass by Benicia's Lake on the right side. This is a nice, shady respite from the climb and during the wetter months, is often filled with chirping frogs and scenic views.

Undulate through the contours of the hills before reaching a trail junction just after a mile. To the right descends Angel's Flight Trail, a shorter loop that will also return you to the trailhead.

For this loop, stay left at this junction instead and continue to the 640-foot summit that hits the peak just after another resting bench. If you timed the weather right, this high point affords you and the kids epic views of the Golden Gate Bridge, so take a moment to look around. Added bonus: It's all downhill from here!

Descend the hillside through a series of trails and staircases, eventually passing a second trail junction that shoots off to the right. That is yet another Shortcut Trail that will return you to the same trailhead but do it in a shorter distance.

The hike downhill passes quickly as you trek through more oak trees and small rock formations. At just over 2 miles, you'll know you're close to the end when you pass the third trail junction of the hike. To the right, you'll see the lower half of the Angel's Flight Trail merge back into the main loop. Once you pass this, you're almost back to the car.

Pass through the trail gate and trek around the back of the Buena Vista Winery. You'll soon find yourself back where you began—and just in time for some wine.

MILES AND DIRECTIONS

0.0   Begin the hike on the trail that leaves from the north side of the parking lot.

0.1   Pass through the gate and begin climbing.

1.1   Arrive at Benicia's Lake.

1.2   Trail junction; stay left.

1.4   Enjoy the moment; you've arrived at the trail's high point.

1.7   Trail junction; stay left.

2.1   Trail junction; stay left.

2.2   Pass the back of the Buena Vista Winery.

2.4   You've arrived back at the car.

21 BODIE GHOST TOWN HIKE

Known as the town frozen in a "state of arrested decay," Bodie is one of the most well-preserved ghost towns in the entire country. With dozens of complete structures, dusty streets, and intact interior furnishings, a hike throughout Bodie is truly a journey back in time.

Start: Bodie Parking Lot
Distance: 0.6 to 6 miles out-and-back
Hiking time: 1 to 3 hours
Difficulty: Easy
Elevation gain: 100 feet
Trail surface: Dirt and rock
Hours open: 9 a.m. to 6 p.m.
Best season: Any season
Water: At Dolan House and between the Dechambeau Hotel and County Barn
Toilets: At the main parking lot and Wheaton & Hollis Hotel
Nursing benches: Picnic tables at Parr House ruins
Stroller-friendly: Yes, some trails

Potential child hazards: The buildings are old.
Other trail users: None
Dogs: Allowed on leash but not in buildings
Land status: California Department of Parks and Recreation
Nearest town: Willow Springs
Fees and permits: Fee
Maps: Bodie State Historic Park brochure
Trail contact: Bodie State Historic Park, CA 270, Bridgeport, CA 93517; (760) 616-5040; www.parks.ca .gov/?page_id=509
Gear suggestions: Sturdy shoes

FINDING THE TRAILHEAD

From Carson City, Nevada, take US 395 south for approximately 85 miles. Turn left onto CA 270 east and go 13 miles. Bodie State Historic Park will be on your right. Park at the main parking lot just off the road and start your tour at Dolan House.

From Modesto, take CA 108 east for 117 miles. Turn left onto CA 270 east and follow the same directions as listed above. GPS: N38 12.79' / W119 0.91'

THE HIKE

It's a voyage down a long, bumpy road to reach the once-prospering community of Bodie, but it's worth every pothole and washboard you encounter (just prepare the kids in advance!).

FUN FACTOR: LAWLESSNESS IN BODIE

At the end of Main Street sits a tiny building that once was the jail for Bodie. Today, it looks oddly small in comparison to the extreme tales of disorderly behavior that took place in town—like the infamous Treloar murder. In 1881, witnesses watched Joseph DeRoche shoot and kill Thomas Treloar as he was leaving a dance at the Union Hall. DeRoche was arrested and placed in the small jail under Constable John Kirgan. But, thanks to Kirgan's temporary demotion, vigilantes removed DeRoche from his cell after midnight and hanged him.

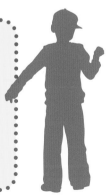

Leaving church on a Sunday

This turned into a fun game of matching the buildings on the map to the buildings in the town.

Another view of the remarkably well-kept structures off the main drag

Bodie isn't like other hikes in this guide since it isn't a typical trail; there is no trailhead and frankly, there is no prescribed route. But that is what makes Bodie the perfect hike for families: There are so many options that you can curate an itinerary that best suits you and your children's needs.

Bodie is a different type of trail because you'll be exploring an entire community. Following the 1849 gold rush, mining prospects plummeted along the western slope of the Sierra Nevada range. Eager for their next gold strike, prospectors traversed the mountains to the eastern slopes, hoping their luck would change. One such prospector was a man named W. S. Bodey who discovered gold in the region in 1859. While he did become the eventual namesake of the entire town, Bodey himself never lived to see it. After striking gold, he died a few months later in a blizzard. These days, his burial site is presumed to be somewhere on the hillside above the Bodie cemetery.

After Bodey's lucky hit, mining continued to gradually progress until a large discovery of gold in 1875 caused the area to boom. As a result, the town of Bodie (now spelled differently) prospered. At its peak, Bodie was the home for more than 7,000 people along with thirty different mines. The town developed a reputation for a rough crowd, so the community grew in kind. With more than sixty saloons along with a number of prostitute "cribs" and opium dens, Bodie was known as a wild place to be.

Of course, we all know how the gold situation eventually ended. As the boom years passed and the mines began to close, the population of Bodie dwindled. Mining continued all the way until 1942, but the population was never as large as it had been during those successful years.

In fact, Bodie became so quiet that the town's last major landowner—a man named James S. Cain—had to hire caretakers to protect the area from looters and vandalism. Ultimately, the state of California purchased the town in 1962 and created the Bodie State Historic Park to preserve the community.

Because of this, you may consider the Bodie Ghost Town hike a "choose your own adventure" of sorts. Regardless of the route, you'll begin at the parking area off Bypass Road and near the restrooms. Walk down the small hill on the paved path and you'll find yourself at the start of Green Street.

For the sake of this guide, we used Green Street as the backbone of our exploration. The mileage detailed walks the length of Green Street, turning around at the Conway House, which is #24 on the Bodie State Historic Park walking guide. If you opt to

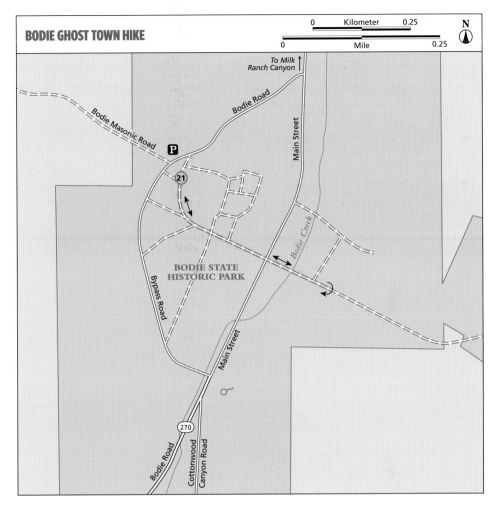

0   Kilometer   0.25

0   Mile   0.25

N

To Milk Ranch Canyon

Bodie Road

Bodie Masonic Road

Main Street

P

21

Bodie Creek

BODIE STATE HISTORIC PARK

Bypass Road

Main Street

270

Bodie Road

Cottonwood Canyon Road

explore the rest of Bodie, you can expect your mileage to be much higher than the 0.6-mile round-trip.

Head south-southeast down Green Street, passing the McDonnell Dolan House on your left before arriving at the Methodist Church. The first notable building on the route, the church was built in 1882 and is the only church still standing in town. A barrier prevents hikers from completely wandering inside, but you can get a good look from the open doorway.

After the church and at 0.1 mile, you'll cross the intersection of Green and Fuller Streets. You'll pass a red barn on the right side that is typical of those seen in Bodie's heyday. Today, the barn still has bits of original red paint visible.

Continue walking on Green Street until you reach the intersection with Prospect Street. On the left side, you'll see a large building that was once the James Stuart Cain house, the same man who was the final owner of Bodie before the state took over. Cain arrived in Bodie in 1879 and immediately embarked upon a lumber business by using nearby Mono Lake to transport goods on large boats. He later became a banker and maintained the Bodie Bank until 1932. While you cannot go inside of Cain's former

Checking out the gym in the O.O.F. Hall

home, the glass window in front has a dazzling display of artifacts that are fun to look at for kids and adults alike.

After Prospect Street, you'll soon arrive at another intersection with Main Street. If your family feels up for adventuring, Main Street is a great option as it leads to many other finds like the Independent Order of Odd Fellows Lodge (and later the Bodie Athletic Club) and the site of Thomas Treloar's murder in 1881 (see sidebar). If not, be sure to take a gander at the small building on the right corner; that's one of two remaining mortuaries in Bodie.

After the intersection with Main Street, you'll find public restrooms on the northwest corner next to the Wheaton and Luhrs Store building.

Nearing the end of Green Street, you'll pass the schoolhouse, the doctor's home, and finally, the former Conway House. Bob Conway is thought to be one of the last residents in Bodie. If you look carefully at the home, you'll still see some green vines growing along the front porch rails. These are hops, and the running joke was that these plants were the only greenery that could survive life in Bodie.

From here, you can turn around and retrace your steps back to the parking lot by walking down the other side of the street. Or, if your family is ready for more, we recommend exploring the length of Main Street, along with the series of small buildings behind the Methodist Church on Fuller Street. There are still a few buildings that are open to the public, and kids love poking through the interior.

MILES AND DIRECTIONS

0.0 Begin in the Bodie State Historic Park main parking lot and find the trail on the southeast corner.

0.1 Trail junction; veer left to turn onto Green Street.

0.2 Trail junction with Main Street; stay straight.

0.3 Reach the Conway House on the left side. Turn around and retrace your steps back to the main lot.

0.6 Arrive back at the main lot.

22 BURST ROCK

This out-of-the-way hike gives you relatively easy access to incredible views of the Sierra. It's well shaded and a nice challenge for young kids who don't quite yet have the stamina for longer hikes but want a reward for their hard work. If you get to the end of the hike and read the sign that explains more about the emigrant trails and Burst Rock history, your kids may gain even more appreciation for how hard it was to travel this country 100+ years ago. Fair warning: The mosquitoes can seem pterodactyl-sized if you happen to time this too close to the hatch, especially if you make it close to any water sources. Check the snowmelt conditions and consider a little later in the summer if you have the choice.

Start: Gianelli trailhead
Distance: 2.6-mile out-and-back
Hiking time: About 3 hours
Difficulty: Easy
Elevation gain: 550 feet
Trail surface: Dirt and rock
Hours open: Dawn to dusk
Best season: Late spring to early winter
Water: None
Toilets: None
Nursing benches: None
Stroller-friendly: No

Potential child hazards: None
Other trail users: None
Dogs: Allowed on leash
Land status: US Forest Service
Nearest town: Pinecrest
Fees and permits: None
Maps: Stanislaus National Forest map
Trail contact: Summit Ranger District, 1 Pinecrest Lake Rd., Pinecrest, CA 95364; (209) 965-3434; www.fs.usda.gov/stanislaus
Gear suggestions: Sturdy shoes

FINDING THE TRAILHEAD

From Modesto, take CA 108 east for approximately 68 miles. Then turn right onto Pinecrest Lake Road and go 0.4 mile. Take a right onto Dodge Ridge Road and go 3.5 miles, then turn right onto Crabtree Road and drive for just over 4 miles until it turns into FR 4N47. Stay on this dirt forest road for 4 miles to the end of the road. Parking is limited but usually not very busy.
GPS: N38 12.07' / W119 52.46'

THE HIKE

The trail sets out from the Gianelli Cabin with little elevation gain as it heads north/northeast toward the edge of the cliffs that peer down into the South Fork of the Stanislaus River. This is a perfect grade for kids who are still getting their hiking legs but also want to feel like they're exploring serious wilderness, as this gets you near the alpine efficiently. After about a mile you'll arrive at the cliffs' edge, where there are fun spots to scramble on large granite boulders as long as your children have a modicum of a sense of self-preservation.

From here the trail bends back to the south, and trends east as it switchbacks its way up toward the summit with Burst Rock. The trail is well maintained and not terribly steep, but you'll certainly feel the 8,200 feet of elevation if you try to push too fast. Most of this section is archetypical Sierra hiking, with patches of granite intermingled with lodgepole

Walking the trail just on the far side of the Burst Rock sign

and other evergreens. The floor is slightly dusty with large patches of needles, making for a relatively comfortable hike and limited obstacles for your little ones to fall on (although we can guarantee our kid will still somehow find the single rock to almost trip over).

Once you come to the Burst Rock sign on the trail, you'll need to take a slight off-trail detour if you want to claim to have actually stood on Burst Rock. This is a short tenth-of-a-mile hike to the overlook, and the edge is steep, high, and entirely unguarded. If you feel safe, you'll have nearly 360 degrees of the High Sierra, complete with views of Castle Rock and the Three Chimneys.

Early morning light looking directly toward Burst Rock

Looking down toward Powell Lake, which is lovely for a swim on hot alpine days

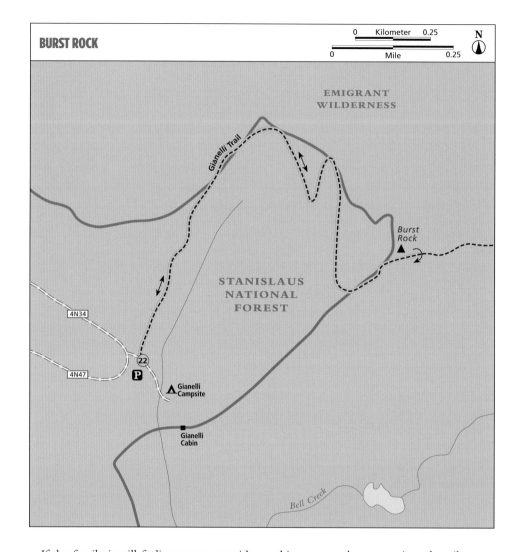

EMIGRANT
WILDERNESS

Gianelli Trail

Burst
Rock
▲
2

STANISLAUS
NATIONAL
FOREST

4N34

22
P
4N47

▲ Gianelli
Campsite

■ Gianelli
Cabin

Bell Creek

0   Kilometer   0.25
N
0   Mile   0.25

If the family is still feeling strong, consider pushing on another approximately mile and a half to Powell Lake. This is mostly downhill from Burst Rock, so keep that in mind when you're considering the return trek, but if you can make it to the lake, it's a wonderful alpine backcountry swimming hole. As you're coming down the hill from Burst Rock, you'll see an unmarked spur at about 2 miles from the original trailhead, and from here you turn north and walk about a third of a mile to Powell Lake. There are plenty of rocks for laying around like a lizard in the sunshine, and the contrast of frigid water and alpine sun makes it fun to hop in and out a few times. There are a few rocky sections that protrude enough for jumping into the lake, but they're not completely clean lines so be sure to spot your kids and double-check the landing before they give it a try.

The overlook from Burst Rock, looking across the South Fork of the Stanislaus River valley

MILES AND DIRECTIONS

0.0 From the parking area, head out on the trail (also called the Gianelli Trail) that heads north.

0.7 Begin a quick series of switchbacks that will carry you up the remainder of the elevation gain.

1.3 You've reached the sign indicating Burst Rock and can see it on the left side of the trail. Turn around and retrace your steps back to the car.

2.6 Arrive back at the parking area.

FUN FACTOR: LEARN ABOUT THE TOUGHEST 4-YEAR-OLD IN HISTORY

The Emigrant Wilderness is named after the emigrant trails established here during the gold rush in the 1850s, and one of the hardiest trails was this specific hike through Emigrant Pass. The Clark-Skidmore party was the first emigrant party to successfully cross the area, and doing so involved raising and lowering their wagons by hand and creating makeshift roads from scratch by manually moving tons of rock. There's an illustration of this on the sign at the base of Burst Rock. The sign also shares a remarkable tale of the birth of Marika Fischer, who was literally born on Burst Rock. Her father built a makeshift shelter here to protect the family during a storm, and while he was off helping other members of the party, his wife went into labor. Naturally they sent their *4-year-old son* into the snow to find help from an Indigenous woman at a nearby camp. He made it successfully, returned with the woman, and Marika was born.

23 **EBBETTS PEAK**

Perched just to the north of Ebbetts Pass with a maximum elevation of 9,188 feet, Ebbetts Peak is a literal pile of rocks that poses a lot of fun for kids of all ages. This adventure is less about hiking and more about climbing, so be prepared to go vertical.

Start: Ebbetts Peak trailhead
Distance: 1.2-mile lollipop loop
Hiking time: About 2 hours
Difficulty: Moderate
Elevation gain: 430 feet
Trail surface: Dirt but mostly rock
Hours open: Dawn to dusk (the road to the trailhead closes in the winter)
Best season: Late spring to early autumn
Water: None
Toilets: None
Nursing benches: None
Stroller-friendly: No

Potential child hazards: Rock scrambles
Other trail users: None
Dogs: Allowed on leash
Land status: US Forest Service
Nearest town: Bear Valley
Fees and permits: None
Maps: Stanislaus National Forest, Mokelumne Wilderness map
Trail contact: Calaveras Ranger District, 5519 CA 4, Hathaway Pines, CA 95233; (209) 795-1381; www.fs .usda.gov/stanislaus
Gear suggestions: Sturdy shoes

FINDING THE TRAILHEAD

From Stockton, take CA 4 east for approximately 114 miles. Then take a sharp left onto FSR 8N04 and go 0.2 mile. If you don't have a high-clearance vehicle, park at the turn onto the Forest Service road. If you do have a high-clearance vehicle, you can likely make it to the upper parking lot a quarter-mile up the dirt road. Parking is very limited. GPS: N39 32.76' / W119 48.68'

THE HIKE

At just over 1 mile round-trip, Ebbetts Peak is one of the shorter hikes included in this guide, but that doesn't make it the easiest. However, most parents can attest to one truth that seems to apply to most children: They want to climb. And this route gives them the opportunity to do just that.

If you arrive in a vehicle with four-wheel drive, you can begin the hike at the small dirt parking spaces near the end of the dirt road that climbs away from the highway. If you don't have a high-clearance vehicle, you'll want to park at the base near CA 4 and hike the quarter-mile up the dirt road. This will add on both length and fatigue for little legs, but it is doable. And it's much better than getting your low-clearance vehicle stuck on the dirt road and hiking to town for help. Choose your battle!

Find the small path on the north side of the parking area and begin hiking uphill as the singletrack winds through a sea of grass, dirt, and rocks. Pro tip: Start slowly. Almost immediately, the route begins to climb and gains more than 150 feet in the first tenth of a mile. It does level out for a little bit, but this quick burst certainly gets the heart rate up for adults and children alike.

Follow the trail as it wraps north-northwest and climbs to just over 9,000 feet. At one-third of a mile, the trail will split with the main route branching left; stay to the right so that you are facing Ebbetts Peak and all of its rocky glory.

Descending off the summit, looking south across the pass

Leaving the main trail and heading toward the summit

Stroll back across the grass toward the shoulder of the big pile of volcanic granite. At roughly 0.5 mile, you'll reach the base of the peak and notice the topography changing from flat grass to large boulders that require climbing. Yes, this is when you can tell your kids that it's time to go up!

You can follow the fairly obvious rock path as it ascends up the shoulder of the peak, but there is no single best way to reach the top. Just be sure to stay behind your kids to help them with proper hand and foot placement on some of the trickier sections. None of the rocks are far apart and most of them are very stable; you won't have to worry about loose boulders. But, if your child is new to this type of terrain, an added hand on her back is always nice for a boost of confidence.

Quite-pregnant Heather descending the volcanic rock off the summit

Soaking in the well-earned views from the summit

Climb for about a quarter-mile and another 100 feet of gain until you reach the top of Ebbetts Peak. You'll know you've arrived at the summit when you reach the American flag that is almost always perched atop the high point. Each year, a group of patriotic hikers ensures Old Glory remains afloat, gently flapping in the breeze for everyone to visit when they arrive.

When you're ready to make the return journey, you have two options. You and your family may return the way you came, but it is longer and will likely add up to more than the given 1.2-mile round-trip distance. Most hikers opt for a direct approach and descend straight down the southwest face of the peak, reaching the parking lot in less than a half of a mile. With careful footing and a general awareness, kids can safely take either route.

FUN FACTOR: END THE DAY WITH SOME SPLASHING

Once your family stands atop Ebbetts Peak, it's time to celebrate! Once you get back to your car, head 30 minutes back down CA 4 where you'll find the main attraction in the Calaveras Ranger District: Lake Alpine. The 180-acre lake sits at 7,300 feet in elevation and boasts more fun than any kid will know what to do with. If hiking is still on the agenda, there is a 4-mile trail around the perimeter. But, if it's a toasty-warm day and everyone is looking to cool off, the crisp water (formed by snowmelt) is the best way to chill out. Swimming, boating, and paddling are all options, as well as fishing the stocked trout or sunbathing. If you love the area enough to stick around for a while, consider booking a cabin or tent-cabin at the family-owned Lake Alpine Lodge, a historic gem of a property. And if not? Swing by and enjoy an evening meal at the character-personified restaurant on-site. We don't know about you, but any establishment that boasts awards like, "The Approval of That One Kid Who We Hear Doesn't Like to Eat Much" deserves a visit.

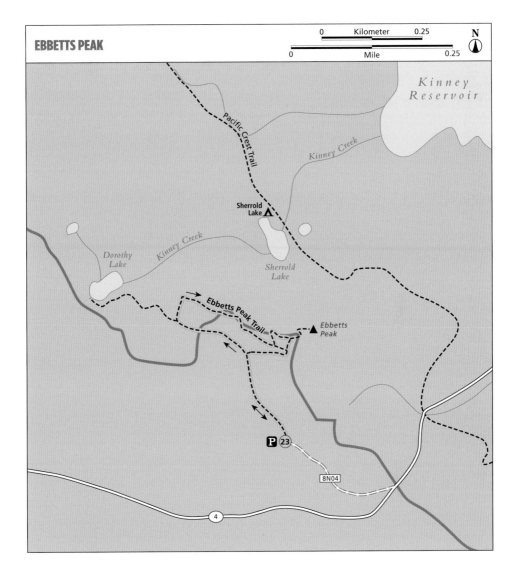

0 Kilometer 0.25

N

0 Mile 0.25

Kinney Reservoir

Pacific Crest Trail

Kinney Creek

Sherrold Lake

Kinney Creek

Dorothy Lake

Sherrold Lake

Ebbetts Peak Trail

Ebbetts Peak

P 23

8N04

4

MILES AND DIRECTIONS

0.0 Begin in the dirt lot at the end of FSR 8N04. Find the small path that leaves from the north side of the parking area.

0.3 Trail junction; stay right and begin ascending the grassy shoulders of the peak.

0.5 Arrive at the rocky base of the peak and begin steeply climbing the scattered boulders.

0.75 You've reached the summit of Ebbetts Peak. Descend the southwest face for the most direct path to your car.

1.2 Arrive back to the parking area.

24 LEAVITT MEADOWS TO LANE LAKE

This is one of those hikes where you feel like you're getting much more than what you paid for. The mild elevation gain and beautiful open meadow make for easy walking, and the sparkling lakes at the conclusion make the perfect spot to pass an afternoon with the family. Bring your fishing rods too; these lakes have plenty of trout that will eagerly take a fly.

Start: Leavitt Meadows trailhead
Distance: 6.5-mile out-and-back
Hiking time: About 6 hours
Difficulty: Moderate
Elevation gain: 400 feet
Trail surface: Dirt and rock
Hours open: Dawn to dusk
Best season: Early spring to early autumn
Water: At Leavitt Meadows campground
Toilets: At Leavitt Meadows campground
Nursing benches: Picnic tables at Leavitt Meadows campground

Stroller-friendly: No
Potential child hazards: None
Other trail users: None
Dogs: Allowed on leash
Land status: US Forest Service
Nearest town: Bridgeport
Fees and permits: None
Maps: Humboldt-Toiyabe National Forest, Hoover Wilderness map
Trail contact: Humboldt-Toiyabe National Forest Bridgeport Ranger District, HC62 Box 1000, Bridgeport, CA 93517; (760) 932-7070; www.fs .usda.gov/htnf
Gear suggestions: Sturdy shoes

FINDING THE TRAILHEAD

From Modesto, take CA 108 east for approximately 111 miles. Turn right into Leavitt Meadows campground and park at the trailhead. Parking is limited. GPS: N38 20.05' / W119 33.11'

THE HIKE

The most complicated navigation is at the start of the hike, where it can be difficult to find the beginning of the trail on the far side of the Leavitt Meadows campground. Once you spot the bridge across the West Fork of the Walker River, you'll know you're in the right place. From there, the trail progresses south along the east side of the river.

The trail begins in a lightly treed area near the campground, but this quickly gives way to open-meadow strolling with mile-long views all the way to your destination. Given the short total distance, it's worth taking a few stops along the river where you can find access via social trails. In late summer, the flows are relatively low enough to be safe for water play.

At about half a mile you'll pass through the junction for the Leavitt Meadow pack station (more on that in the sidebar); continue heading south on the West Walker River Trail for another mile until you come to another junction. Stay south again, and begin the mile-long climb up toward Lane Lake. Most of the hike's elevation gain is in this mile-long stretch, so take plenty of breaks, as once you hit about 7,500 feet you'll have clear views down to Roosevelt Lake. From here drop about 250 feet in elevation and you'll arrive at Roosevelt Lake, with Lane Lake just a few hundred feet beyond.

Looking down on Leavitt Meadows from the roadside overlook

If you have time for a lazy day, it's worth regular stops by the river to cool off.

Much of the trail tracks through open meadow like this—bring sun protection!

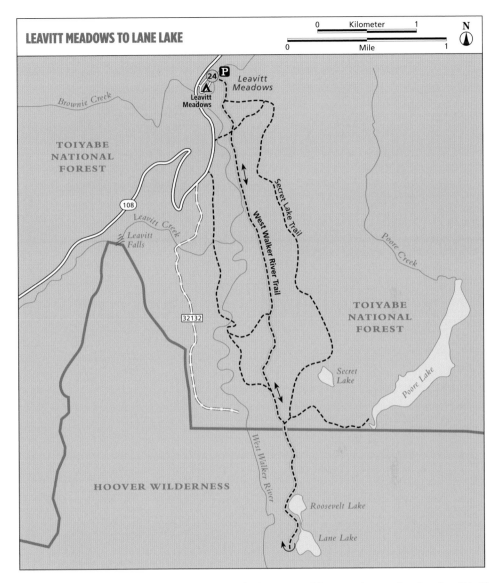

Fishing in both lakes is excellent, and it's a reasonably easy place to hook a few fish if your kids are still learning. You'd be entitled to spend the rest of the day here, but if you still have the energy, there are a few spots nearby worth some exploration.

There's a small cascade about a mile south of Lane Lake. Take the horse trail that turns south/southeast after you get to the far side of Lane Lake, and continue tracking alongside the river until you arrive at the falls. Another option involves backtracking to the junction at the peak trail elevation around 7,500 feet and heading northeast to Secret Lake. There's great fishing here too, and if you want some variation on your return trip, you may continue on this trail to the north and it will eventually drop you down into Leavitt Meadows Campground. This Secret Lake Trail runs along the ridgeline and offers nice views into the Leavitt Meadows Valley, and if you go during the buggy season, we've found this trail slightly less mosquito-infested than the West Walker River Trail.

Finally, this hike makes an excellent introduction to backcountry camping. The low mileage and low elevation change make for a manageable day, and with plenty of water available you can save some pack weight. Plus you can use the Lane Lake area as a basecamp, so if you'd like to spend a couple of nights, there's plenty to explore toward Fremont Lake with a lighter pack.

Playing in the river—one of the many ways a short hike turns into an all-day affair

MILES AND DIRECTIONS

0.0 Begin hiking on the trail on the north side of Leavitt Meadows Campground.

0.2 Trail junction; stay right.

0.4 Trail intersection; stay straight and continue skirting along the east side of Leavitt Meadow.

1.6 Begin your ascent up to the trail's high point.

2.4 Trail junction; stay right.

2.5 Begin descending toward Roosevelt Lake.

2.8 You've reached the north shore of Roosevelt Lake. Follow the trail as it curves westward and skirts the perimeter of the lake.

3.0 You've reached the in-between south of Roosevelt and north of Lane Lake.

3.2 You've arrived at Lane Lake. Hike along the western shore to find a good picnic spot or campsite. Whenever you're done with your adventure, turn around and retrace your steps.

6.5 Arrive back at the campground.

FUN FACTOR: PACK TRIPS

One of the biggest challenges of traveling with kids is all the *stuff* that a tiny human requires for regular living, and this challenge is no different in the backcountry. One way to make your life a little easier: horsepacking. The Leavitt Meadows Pack Station (located near the trailhead at the Leavitt Meadows Campground) offers a dunnage drop for your gear so you may hike relatively unburdened while the pack animals cart in your cast-iron stove for family breakfasts. This is particularly useful for the age where children are a bit too big for a full day in a kid carrier but not strong enough to log more than a few miles. If your family is comfortable on horseback, you also have the option to ride into your campground along with your gear; this is one of the most memorable ways to get into the backcountry without the usual burden of lugging all of your own stuff.

California's most popular park boasts some of the state's most iconic attractions. On that list is Yosemite Falls, but families with young children are often thwarted in hiking the trail since it takes more than 2,700 feet of climbing to arrive at the top. Enter Lower Yosemite Falls Trail, a manageable 1-mile-long journey to the base of Lower Yosemite Falls that is doable by almost any child or adult.

Start: Lower Yosemite Falls trailhead
Distance: 1.2-mile loop
Hiking time: About 1 hour
Difficulty: Easy
Elevation gain: 50 feet
Trail surface: Dirt
Hours open: Open daily, 24 hours a day
Best season: Early spring to late autumn
Water: At the trailhead
Toilets: At the trailhead
Nursing benches: Picnic tables at the trailhead
Stroller-friendly: Yes

Potential child hazards: None
Other trail users: None
Dogs: Not allowed
Land status: National Park Service
Nearest town: Yosemite
Fees and permits: Fee to enter the park, or purchase America the Beautiful annual pass
Maps: Yosemite National Park map
Trail contact: Yosemite National Park, PO Box 577, Yosemite, CA 95389; (209) 372-0200; www.nps .gov/yose
Gear suggestions: Sturdy shoes

FINDING THE TRAILHEAD

From San Francisco, take I-580 east for approximately 45 miles. Keep left to continue onto I-205 east for 15 miles following signs for Tracy/Stockton. Merge onto I-5 north briefly and then take exit 461 for CA 120 toward Manteca/ Sonora. Stay on CA 120 for approximately 92 miles. Turn right onto Big Oak Flat Road and go 10 miles, and then turn left onto El Portal Road. El Portal Road turns slightly right and becomes Southside Drive. Stay on Southside Drive for 4.2 miles and then take a left onto Sentinel Drive. Take the next left onto Northside Drive and park on your left in the large parking lot. This is one of the most popular trails in Yosemite National Park, so parking is very limited. GPS: N37 44.79' / W119 35.78'

THE HIKE

Yosemite Falls is the tallest waterfall in North America, rising more than 2,425 feet from the Yosemite Valley floor. There, a winter's worth of snowmelt seeps into Yosemite Creek as it drains an area that's nearly 50 square miles in size. The frothy cascade thunders toward Yosemite Falls, first reaching Upper Falls where it plunges 1,430 feet (more than half of the total drop) over the edge of a hanging valley before it reaches the middle section, known as the Middle Cascades. Here, a series of four smaller plunges combine for a drop total of 675 feet, but this region is tough to observe from any of the lookouts so it's rarely noted.

Finally, the water flows toward Lower Yosemite Falls where it pours over the edge to drop a final 320 feet into the pool below. From here, the water flows into the Merced River and continues its journey toward the San Joaquin River in the Central Valley.

Enjoying one of the beautiful valley campgrounds near the trailhead

Approaching the base of the falls

Morning views of the Upper and Lower Falls

The trail to Upper Yosemite Falls is known to be one of the park's oldest historic trails (dating back to the 1870s), but it is a challenging hike that ascends a few thousand feet and takes most of a day. However, there is still a good way to see the falls and enjoy a hike—even for the littles in the group.

Lower Yosemite Falls is one of the most popular attractions in the park, and for good reason. The viewing bridge that sits at the base of Lower Yosemite is so close that visitors will feel the mist from the falls as it drips down their skin. And this mellow hike rewards

Sunrise near the trailhead

trekkers with stunning views of both the Upper and Lower Falls, so no one misses anything. Finally, the entire loop is comprised of two paved paths with a total of 100 feet in elevation change. This means that anyone—even family members that may need a wheelchair—can catch a glimpse of the sparkling water by using the eastern portion of the loop as a simple out-and-back.

Beginning at the Lower Yosemite Falls Trailhead off Northside Drive, hop on the easily identifiable paved path that heads north directly toward the falls. You can hike the loop in either direction but doing it clockwise affords you the best views of the waterfalls.

As you're hiking, consider stopping at any of the exhibits along the way. Set up by the Park Service, these exhibits educate visitors on a number of topics regarding the culture and nature of the region. You'll pass by one such exhibit—*Shaping Yosemite Valley*—on the right side at 0.2 mile.

Continue hiking northward, following the clear, defined walkway as it heads toward the Lower Falls. The water gets closer and closer, and you'll begin hearing the thunderous crash of rapids as you near the viewing bridge. It feels exciting!

At 0.3 mile, you'll arrive at the viewing bridge that takes you as close to the Lower Falls as you'll get on this hike. The misty water will soak through everybody's hair, but it's a real treat on hot summer afternoons. Once you've soaked in the view (pun intended!), follow the walking path as it trends eastward, eventually turning south back toward the trailhead at mile 0.5.

From there, it's easy going all the way back. The views on the east side of the loop aren't as spectacular, so many hikers opt to just hike the west side as an out-and-back. Because of this, there are noticeably fewer people on the east side of the loop (although that's a relative measurement in Yosemite).

FUN FACTOR: BECOME A JUNIOR RANGER

It's possible for kids to become Junior Rangers at any national park, but bearing the name from Yosemite National Park garners a special level of awe. And, with 27,000 kids becoming Junior Rangers every year, it's clearly a coveted designation!

To help your kids earn this moniker, buy a self-guided activity book at any of the visitor centers or information stations. They're only a few dollars. Then, your kiddos must complete the education activities in the book, pick up a bag of trash in the park, and attend a ranger-guided program. Once they've done those three things, you can return to the visitor center so your children can receive their special acknowledgment. The Junior Ranger program is geared toward kids ages 7 to 13, but children ages 3 to 6 can also participate with the Little Cub Handbook.

At 0.7 mile, you'll see a small trail that jets off to the right. Turn right and head over to the Falls View. This is worth a few extra steps to see the zoomed-out version of the falls.

Return back to the main path and turn westward (toward the right) at mile 1.0. Now, you're hiking parallel to the main road, and you'll follow this all the way back to the trailhead.

There's plenty of opportunity to watch for wildlife after your hike wraps.

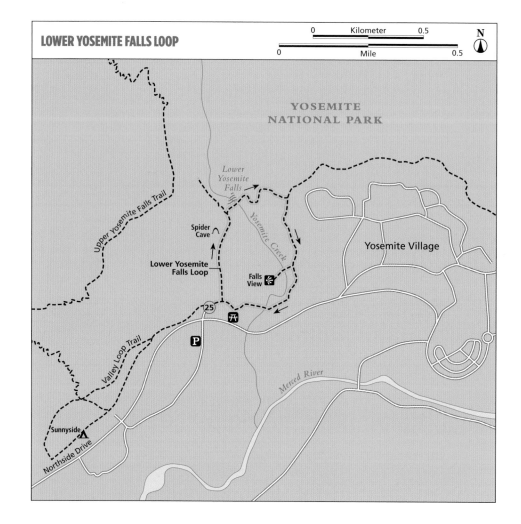

LOWER YOSEMITE FALLS LOOP

YOSEMITE NATIONAL PARK

Lower Yosemite Falls

Spider Cave

Lower Yosemite Falls Loop

Falls View

Yosemite Village

Yosemite Creek

Upper Yosemite Falls Trail

Valley Loop Trail

Merced River

Sunnyside

Northside Drive

MILES AND DIRECTIONS

0.0 Begin at the Lower Yosemite Falls Trailhead on Northside Drive.

0.1 Turn left and hike north to enjoy the loop in a clockwise direction.

0.2 Trail junction; stay straight.

0.3 Reach the viewing bridge at the base of the Lower Falls. This is a popular spot to snap a photo!

0.4 You'll pass a small exhibit entitled *John Muir: The Woodcutter*.

0.5 Trail junction; stay right. The trail to the left is the North Valley Trail.

0.7 Turn right to head down the short spur trail that ends at the Falls Overlook.

1.0 A small spur trail turns left; stay straight to return to the trailhead. Or, turn left and head back out onto the bike path.

1.2 You've reached the trailhead.

26 MCGHEE CREEK CANYON

McGhee has it all: funky rock formations, doable terrain, and a babbling creek that may or may not roar depending on the time of year you visit. The distance can appear long for families with younger children, but that's the beauty of this hike: You can turn around at any point and you'll still be dazzled by all the Eastern Sierra has to offer.

Start: McGhee Pass trailhead
Distance: 5.6-mile out-and-back
Hiking time: About 6 hours
Difficulty: Moderate to strenuous
Elevation gain: 1,004 feet
Trail surface: Dirt and rock
Hours open: Dawn to dusk
Best season: Late spring to early autumn
Water: Treated at creeks and lakes
Toilets: At the trailhead
Nursing benches: None
Stroller-friendly: No

Potential child hazards: Stream crossings
Other trail users: None
Dogs: Allowed on leash
Land status: US Forest Service
Nearest town: Mammoth Lakes
Fees and permits: None
Maps: Inyo National Forest, Mammoth Lakes Area map
Trail contact: Inyo National Forest, 351 Pacu Ln., Ste. 200, Bishop, CA 93514; (760) 873-2400; www.fs.usda .gov/inyo
Gear suggestions: Sturdy shoes

FINDING THE TRAILHEAD

From Modesto, take CA 120 east for approximately 110 miles until the road ends at a T-stop. Take a right onto US 395 south for 33.5 miles. Turn right onto McGhee Creek Road and drive approximately 3 miles. Parking is limited and usually busy during peak fall foliage. GPS: N37 33.05' / W118 48.18'

THE HIKE

This hike is photogenic no matter what time of year you visit. But, it's one of the few hikes in this guide that truly shines in autumn when the twinkling aspen leaves glitter gold in the sunlight and fill the hillsides with a neon pop of color.

The hike gets started just after the McGhee Creek Pack Station, which can often provide entertainment for the kids on its own. The Pack Station offers High Sierra pack trips via horse and mule rides, so it's possible that you'll witness a string of animals heading out or returning from a backcountry adventure. Give the animals space, but seeing these four-legged friends roam around is often a highlight for our younger kids.

From the beginning, you'll notice a few options for trails, but they all head to the same place and will reconvene by 0.9 mile. Start hiking on a meandering incline that is noticeable but doable. This continues until your turnaround point, so remind your children that slow and steady wins the race. We don't want to burn out! The ascent wraps through a series of low-growing chaparral and sagebrush, the latter of which fills the air with its sharp and earthy scent.

While steadily working uphill, take a look around to admire the multitude of vegetation native to the area. To your right, you'll notice scraggy and gnarled juniper trees clinging to the slope, and to your left are a grove of tenacious aspen trees trending

Opening views look up toward the Sierra Crest

Summertime runoff can make some of the creek crossings a little challenging.

If you're comfortable on a horse, this is a nice alternative for exploring McGhee Creek.

noticeably toward the creekbed. Ahead, admire panoramic views of Mount Aggie and Mount Baldwin, the latter which crests just over 12,000 feet.

At just over 1.0 mile, you'll pass into the John Muir Wilderness Area, marked with a wooden sign. Here, the trail turns toward the south as it runs parallel to McGhee Creek. This section offers one of the more spectacular views in the fall since aspen fill the surrounding hillsides. If you visit in early October, there is a great chance you'll see the full spectrum of autumnal colors, ranging from golden yellow to blazing red.

FUN FACTOR: GONE FISHING

Just 40 minutes away from the McGhee Creek Trailhead sits Crowley Lake, a 12-mile-long and 5-mile-wide lake known as one of the best fisheries in the western United States. Created nearly 7,000 years ago by a massive volcanic eruption that sent lava and debris flowing into the area, the now-lakebed became a massive meadow. Then, Los Angeles built the Long Meadow Dam in 1941, subsequently creating Crowley Lake. With more than 45 miles of shoreline, it's one of the few areas where visitors can drive their vehicles right up to the edge, making it accessible for almost anyone. These days, it's famous for its trout, but water activities like boating, kayaking, waterskiing, and paddleboarding are also popular. And there are lakeside cabins available for families who want to spend a few nights playing on the water.

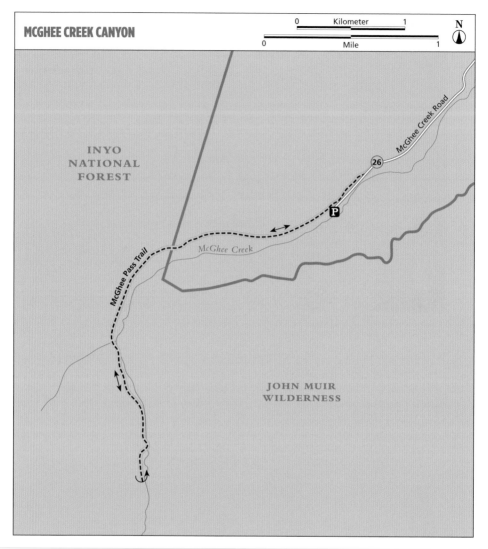

If your children are tired, this view after 1.1 miles is the first option for a decent turn-around point. But if there is still gas left in the tank, press onward!

Climb higher until you reach a heavier creek around 1.7 miles. Depending on the drought conditions and level of water, you may have to boulder hop to get across the water. Once you do, you'll notice a small-but-steep spur trail that juts out toward the left to McGhee Creek. If a rest is needed for everyone, this is our recommendation for a brief relaxation point.

The trail steadily wraps south as the elevation relentlessly yet consistently climbs. You'll pass through a few more aspen groves, but be sure to look above you to the right. Here, a long ridgeline between Mount Crocker and Mount Stanford paints a pretty picture to look at.

Hike a bit farther and you'll reach an odd V-shaped bridge stretching over McGhee Creek at 2.8 miles. The wooden bridge is constructed with two large boards that dip

Checking out one of the washed-out bridges

into the creek and then back out again as the trail continues on along the east bank of the water. Of course, you can certainly continue onward, but for the sake of our included mileage, this is your turnaround point. Retrace your steps to return back to the trailhead.

MILES AND DIRECTIONS

0.0 The trail itself begins just past the McGhee Backpacker Campground, just past the Pack Station.

0.7 The myriad of trails splits begin here, but they all run parallel to each other and reconvene shortly.

0.9 The braided trails merge back onto the singular McGhee Creek Trail.

1.0 The trail turns south and a sign indicates you've entered into the John Muir Wilderness Area.

1.7 Cross through the creek to stay on the trail.

2.1 A small spur trail heads to the right; stay straight.

2.8 A wooden bridge crosses McGhee Creek; turn around and retrace your steps.

5.6 Arrive back at the trailhead.

27 METHUSELAH TRAIL

Situated between 10,000 and 11,000 feet, the Methuselah National Recreation Loop Trail isn't topographically difficult (there's minimal elevation gain) but more than makes up for it with its call for high-altitude lungs. If your kids need a little encouragement, let them know that one of the oldest trees in the world lives in this grove in a secret location!

Start: Methuselah trailhead
Distance: 4.0-mile lollipop loop
Hiking time: About 5 hours
Difficulty: Moderate
Elevation gain: 900 feet
Trail surface: Dirt and rock
Hours open: 6 a.m. to 10 p.m.
Best season: Spring to autumn
Water: At the trailhead
Toilets: At the trailhead
Nursing benches: None
Stroller-friendly: No
Potential child hazards: None
Other trail users: None

Dogs: Allowed on leash
Land status: US Forest Service
Nearest town: Lone Pine
Fees and permits: Fee per person with max per car, but kids under 18 free
Maps: Inyo National Forest, Methuselah area map
Trail contact: Inyo National Forest, 351 Pacu Ln., Ste. 200, Bishop, CA 93514; (760) 873-2400; www.fs.usda.gov/inyo
Gear suggestions: Sturdy shoes and sunscreen (there is little to no shade)

FINDING THE TRAILHEAD

From Bakersfield, take CA 58 east for approximately 55 miles. Take exit 167 to Highway 14 toward Bishop/Mojave and go 46 miles. Continue onto US 395 north for 107 miles and then turn right onto CA 168 east for approximately 13 miles. Turn left onto White Mountain Road and go 10 miles until you reach the Ancient Bristlecone Pine Forest Visitor Center (you'll know it when you reach the end of the paved road). Parking is usually easy to find at the visitor center, and the trailhead is behind the visitor center. GPS: N37 23.02' / W118 10.79'

THE HIKE

Oxygen is scarce above 10,000 feet, but bristlecone trees don't seem to mind at all. In fact, this gnarled and twisted ancient tree seems to prefer life perched on an isolated windswept ridge high above the ground in Inyo National Forest. Core-shaking winds and blustery-cold temperatures whip through the region with a ferocity that shakes humans. And yet, the bristlecone trees continue to survive—and thrive.

For children especially, trekking around these twisted and coiled limbs sparks a mixed experience wrought with equal parts of delight and horror. We can never predict the shape of the pines since their limbs are gnarled in such odd positions that they seem to stretch away from the trunks, almost as if they are human arms reaching for the sky. Some of the pines are fat and squat, while others are lean and lithe as they twist like corkscrews toward the clouds. Regardless of the shape, the bristlecone often remind children of a fantasy world found in *Alice in Wonderland*, or even Dr. Seuss.

More surprising? One would assume these ancient trees are as scarred and rough to the touch as they are wizened and coiled to the eyes. But, in reality, bristlecone trees are

Sunset from the trail looking toward the Sierra Crest

surprisingly smooth. Thanks to the gusty winds that sweep through the groves, pebbles and bits of ice grind up against the tree trunks, constantly polishing the bark into a glass-like surface. Ask your child to gently touch the bark and we're willing to bet that she will be surprised at the tactile experience she discovers.

But the real magic of bristlecone pine trees isn't in their appearance, or even their environment. Instead, the sorcery of these special trees exists in their fearfully slow growth rate. Some believe the terrifying weather conditions slow the growth of these trees, but that appears to be a good thing. Often, the pines grow so slow that they don't even add a single ring to their trunk over an entire year, and for some, it may take over 100 years to expand the trunk an inch in diameter.

Because of this, bristlecone trees are as sneakily deceptive as a toddler with stolen sweets. If you spot a tiny sapling on the side of the trail, it may be easy to assume the tree is just a baby. However, it is quite possible that the little fellow is hundreds of years old and simply taking his time on the growth chart.

Therein lies the secret to the trees' longevity. Because they grow so slowly, their trunks have plenty of time to grow dense and sturdy, almost as if they are wrapping the core of the tree in an impenetrable fortress of bark. Neither bugs nor fungi can break through the wall of protection, and it's not uncommon to see a dead tree standing upright for hundreds of years, its petrified trunk still fighting off rot.

Of course, the best way to visit these special trees is by hiking the trail. And to do that, you must begin at the Ancient Bristlecone Pine Forest Visitor Center. Follow the well-marked signs for "Methuselah Walk" to get started.

Immediately, the trail slightly dips but will soon begin climbing. At 0.2 mile, you'll come across a sign asking you to stay to the right; you are now embarking up on the loop trail. The route to your left is the path you will return on to close the loop.

The trail is mostly exposed and rocky, so the best features are the gnarled bristlecone.

Continue hiking upward until mile 0.5 when you'll reach the top of the first small hill. Congratulations: You've now reached the highest point on the trail! You'll know you've arrived at the high point by the bench sitting on the summit. Relax a moment and soak in the views.

From this bench, the trail slowly turns south as it descends for a quarter-mile. At 0.8 mile, you'll come across a trail junction with Cabin Trail; stay straight to stay on the Methuselah Loop. Continue hiking downward as the trail gradually turns east.

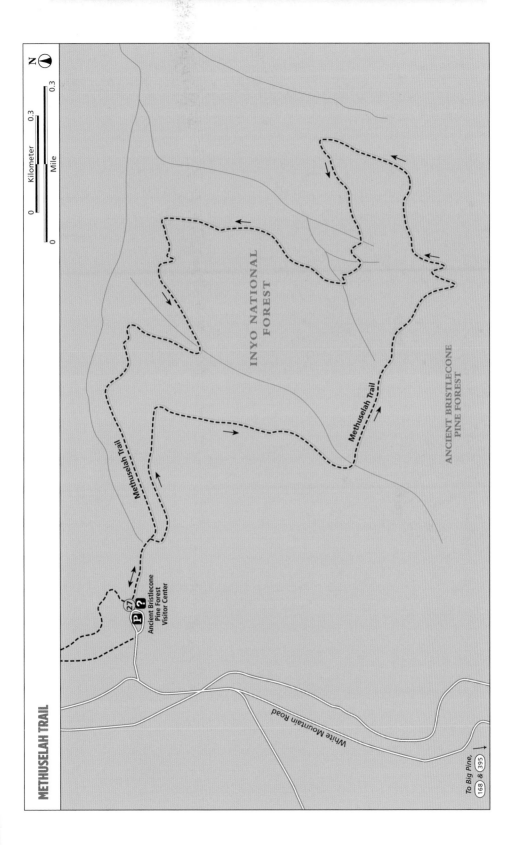

METHUSELAH TRAIL

INYO NATIONAL FOREST

ANCIENT BRISTLECONE PINE FOREST

Methuselah Trail

Ancient Bristlecone Pine Forest Visitor Center

White Mountain Road

To Big Pine, 168 & 395

N

Kilometer
0   0.3   0.3
Mile

Early evening Milky Way with nice sidelight from the setting moon

FUN FACTOR: PROMETHEUS

Methuselah is surely an old tree, and until 2013, it was thought to be the oldest tree in the world. Now we know that another (unnamed) tree has taken the crown from Methuselah as the oldest on earth. But prior to either of these two bristlecone pines, there was Prometheus.

In 1964, a graduate student named Ronald Rusk Currey was studying climate dynamics of the Little Ice Age using tree-ring dating techniques. He studied some of the trees in the Great Basin bristlecone population (not realizing it had already been studied) and became convinced he was analyzing some very old trees. He began taking core samples and grew interested in a tree he named WPN-114, or Prometheus. He continually tried to take core samples with a 28-inch borer but kept breaking the borers or getting them stuck. Finally, he requested permission from the US Forest Service to cut the tree down so he could examine the trunk. The tree was deemed insignificant, the request was granted, and it was only after Prometheus was felled that everyone realized it was the oldest tree ever discovered at that point in time. If it still existed today, it would be 50 years older than Methuselah.

Silver lining: While tragic for Prometheus (and science), this experience led to tighter restrictions on tree cutting. And, this is also why the identity of Methuselah has been forever kept secret.

Soon you'll hike into an area known as the Sculpture Garden, unique since the harsh weather has molded the bristlecone pines into weird and odd shapes. With kids, it's fun to look at the artistic formations and play a guessing game as to what it looks like the most.

Continue hiking onto the back section of the loop, passing through Methuselah Grove, home to one of the oldest trees in the world (and the namesake of this loop). Named Methuselah, the tree is unidentified for fear that bandits or vandalizers will cut down the tree for gain. Have some fun guessing which tree you think it is!

Just after this, you'll hit the lowest point on the trail at 9,586 feet. From here, you'll begin the climb out (roughly 500 feet of gain) to return to close the loop and return to the trailhead.

MILES AND DIRECTIONS

0.0   Start in the parking lot of the Ancient Bristlecone Pine Forest Visitor Center.

0.2   Reach the sign asking you to stay to the right.

0.5   You've topped out at the high point of the trail.

0.8   Trail junction with Cabin Trail; stay straight.

1.4   The trail turns east.

2.3   You've reached the Sculpture Garden.

2.4   Now you will enter Methuselah Grove.

2.8   The low point on the trail.

4.0   You are back in the parking lot.

A fun game to play with the kids—what shapes do you see in this tree?

28 **MINARET VISTA LOOP**

Adults may call this loop a viewpoint, but the short distance and flat terrain combine to make the Minaret Vista Loop a family-friendly hike that's more than a simple overlook. For younger children who may not yet be able to hike into the alpine to witness the dramatic skyline of the Eastern Sierra, this quick loop trail gives them that opportunity. One tip: Don't forget your camera!

Start: Minaret Summit trailhead
Distance: 0.25-mile loop
Hiking time: About 30 minutes
Difficulty: Easy
Elevation gain: 20 feet
Trail surface: Dirt and rock
Hours open: Dawn to dusk (road to the trailhead closes in the winter)
Best season: Late spring to early autumn
Water: None
Toilets: At the trailhead
Nursing benches: Picnic tables at the trailhead

Stroller-friendly: No
Potential child hazards: None
Other trail users: None
Dogs: Allowed on leash
Land status: US Forest Service
Nearest town: Mammoth Lakes
Fees and permits: None
Maps: Inyo National Forest, Mammoth Lakes Area map
Trail contact: Inyo National Forest, 351 Pacu Ln., Ste. 200, Bishop, CA 93514; (760) 873-2400; www.fs.usda .gov/inyo
Gear suggestions: Sturdy shoes

FINDING THE TRAILHEAD

From Modesto, take CA 120 east for approximately 110 miles until the road ends at a T-stop. Take a right onto US 395 south and go 20 miles. Turn right onto Mammoth Scenic Loop and drive 6 miles, and then take another right onto Minaret Road and go 4.5 miles. Take a right at the Entrance Station to head up to the Minaret summit. Parking is limited at the summit. GPS: N37 38.52' / W119 1.83'

THE HIKE

Mammoth and its accompanying world–class ski resort are known worldwide for unparalleled beauty in a magnificent mountain range. But often, the more well-known hikes in the area involve larger climbs and full days on the mountain that don't always work with the littles in tow. If you're looking for a quick adventure for the youngest in your group or simply want to add on to a longer hike by tacking on some bonus scenery, the Minaret Vista Loop is the trek for you.

The trail begins and ends at the Minaret Vista and parking area. The beginning of the trail is easy enough to find, and you'll be hiking in a loop. You can go in either direction, but for the sake of this description, we'll head clockwise.

The trail gently descends almost immediately, but it's a quick drop with a small 35 feet of elevation lost. The small dirt path continues northward, but take a look to the left and you'll see both Mount Ritter (13,157 feet) and Banner Peak (12,945 feet) off in the distance. As the two tallest peaks in the range, their silhouettes are quite remarkable. To the south, you'll see the distinct and iconic jagged ridgeline of the Minarets. These lofty granite pinnacles have a remarkable shape that is recognizable anywhere. While they

These may be the easiest high-country views you'll earn.

Prep the post-hike picnic and enjoy gorgeous views when you wrap the hike.

Morning backlight on the wildflowers that cover the start of the trail

aren't as tall as Banner or Ritter behind them (they clock in around 12,200 feet), their tooth-like appearance is almost more impressive against a bluebird skyline.

After soaking in the magnificent view, follow the trail as it wraps back toward the parking area. As you near the end, you'll see a series of picnic tables to the left. If you packed snacks or a lunch, we can think of no better location to sit down and enjoy a meal with your family. Just beyond the picnic area sits the Minaret Summit (9,266 feet), a small-yet-fun summit to run up and tag.

FUN FACTOR: TAKE A TOUR OF MAMMOTH

The mountain town of Mammoth was practically made for families. For starters, the on-mountain Adventure Center boasts a number of activities that please kids of all ages. Options include a ropes course, bungee trampoline, a climbing wall, a junior zipline, a pump track for little bikers, and even Woolly's Mining Co., a mining experience that allows kids to get their hands into the mix in the hopes of striking it rich.

Beyond the Adventure Center, Mammoth offers plenty of other kid-friendly fun like horseback riding and even more rock climbing. And if the fam is famished after a day packed full of adventure, head down to Main Street in Mammoth Lakes (the main thoroughfare) and find kid-approved culinary delights like enchiladas at Gomez's Restaurant or made-to-order pizza at Giovanni's.

The wide, well-maintained trail makes for lovely family strolling.

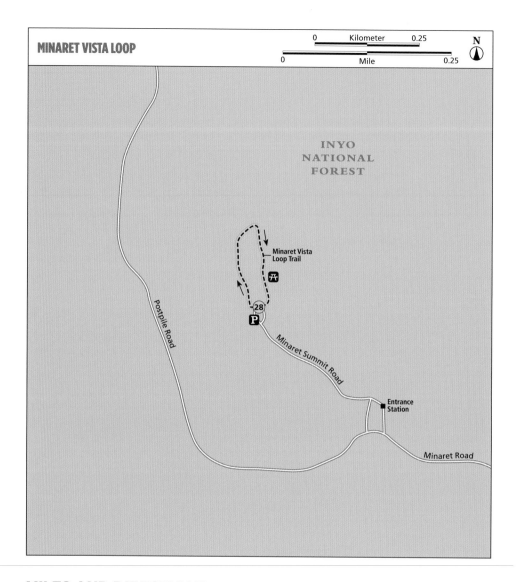

MILES AND DIRECTIONS

0.0   Begin the hike in the Minaret Vista Parking area.

0.1   Look out to the left to catch a glimpse of the Minarets, Banner Peak, and Mount Ritter.

0.15 The trail turns south back toward the parking lot.

0.2   Pass the picnic area on the left side.

0.25 Return to the parking area.

29 NATURAL BRIDGES TRAIL

From the road, this unassuming, dusty, and often hot trail feels like it won't be worth your time or energy. But, if you put in the work to get to the end, you'll be rewarded with a world-class swimming hole and unique geological formations that craft one memorable experience. Don't forget your floaties!

Start: Natural Bridges trailhead
Distance: 2.1-mile out-and-back
Hiking time: 2 hours
Difficulty: Easy
Elevation gain: 380 feet
Trail surface: Dirt and rock
Hours open: Dawn to dusk
Best season: Summer
Water: None
Toilets: At the trailhead
Nursing benches: Picnic bench at the mouth of the cavern
Stroller-friendly: No
Potential child hazards: Stream crossings
Other trail users: None

Dogs: Not allowed
Land status: US Bureau of Reclamation
Nearest town: Vallecito
Fees and permits: Fee per vehicle
Maps: US Bureau of Reclamation Natural Bridges Trail map
Trail contact: US Bureau of Reclamation New Melones Recreation and Resources Branch, 6850 Studhorse Flat Rd., Sonora, CA 95370; (209) 536-9094; www.usbr.gov/mp/ccao/newmelones
Gear suggestions: Sturdy shoes, bathing suit, and water tube to float on

FINDING THE TRAILHEAD

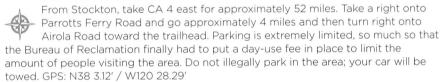

From Stockton, take CA 4 east for approximately 52 miles. Take a right onto Parrotts Ferry Road and go approximately 4 miles and then turn right onto Airola Road toward the trailhead. Parking is extremely limited, so much so that the Bureau of Reclamation finally had to put a day-use fee in place to limit the amount of people visiting the area. Do not illegally park in the area; your car will be towed. GPS: N38 3.12' / W120 28.29'

THE HIKE

Yosemite Valley or Sequoia National Park and its magnificent trees are known worldwide thanks to their utter magnitude and sheer beauty. But those aren't the only spots worth visiting. While Natural Bridges Trail may not be popular outside of Calaveras County, we'd argue it ranks right up there with some of the nationally ranked natural wonders in this country.

That's not to say you'll find utter solitude and tranquility on this trail; quite the opposite, in fact. Natural Bridges is easily one of the most popular hikes in the county. On our midweek visit in August, we were merely one of a half-dozen groups enjoying the water hole. As a result, the local tourism board has enacted a "Know Before You Go" campaign to protect this fragile ecosystem. Neither dogs nor bikes are allowed. If you show up to find the parking area full, the county highly recommends you enjoy any of the other water-filled hikes in the region. And, of course, always be sure to pack out any trash or items you carry in.

All that said, the juice is worth the squeeze. We promise!

Hiking down is the easy part—we definitely had to carry her back up on the way out.

Plan on spending four times as long here as you spent hiking.

When driving in on Parrotts Ferry Road, look for the brown sign on the west side that says "Natural Bridges Day Use Area" next to a small paved road (known as Airola Road on Google Maps). That's your turn.

Parking is limited along the quarter-mile-long paved road, so it's best to get there early or visit midweek. Once your car is safely stashed away, look for the round metal gate back near the junction of the parking lot and Parrotts Ferry Road. The gate is designed to keep bikes off the trail, so it is tough to miss.

The singletrack runs parallel to Parrotts Ferry, almost immediately beginning its steep descent. Enjoy the brief shade in a tree-lined ravine before crossing a wooden bridge and reaching a junction with a forest road at 0.15 mile. Turn right.

The hike continually descends on widening trails, passing through a series of brush that includes oak trees and chamise, a flowering plant native to California. At 0.3 mile, you'll pass a picnic table which makes for a great spot to rest tired legs (especially on the return climb!).

After a few more minutes, the trail breaks free of the shrub and you'll realize that the old stage road is now traversing the side of a canyon created by Coyote Creek. Pass another small trail junction on the right at 0.6 mile, but stay to the left. The other direction is a lesser-used route that will return you back up to the trailhead.

At 0.7 mile, the trail turns sharply to the left as you begin the final descent into the creekbed. You'll hear the water rushing as you get closer to the bottom, but you'll know you're almost there when you encounter a metal sign on the right side of the trail. The plaque gives visitors a glimpse into the area's history and reads:

> *This Natural Bridge was acquired in 1972 for the public as part of the New Melones Lake project through the cooperation and generosity of Tome M. and Margaret E. Airola, members of a pioneer Calaveras County cattle-raising family. Mr. Airola's grandfather, Emmanuel Airola, a native of Italy, immigrated to the town of Melones, located on the Stanislaus River a few miles south of this Natural Bridge, in 1860. In the cattle business for over 75 years, Tome M. Airola grazed cattle in this area as a small boy.*

Descend down a steep set of stairs made with railroad ties, pass by yet another picnic area, and arrive at the small unassuming stream. But, before you count it out, look upstream and you'll see a beautiful limestone cave shrouded in verdant mossy rocks and sparkling water droplet. Pro tip: Now is a good time to tell your kids you've reached Fern Gully!

Hike below the bridge and into the "mouth" of the cave to find a spectacular, semi-hidden swimming hole protected by the limestone overhang. Small children can play in the shallow end, but the water does get deeper as it moves toward the back of the cave. Shallow or not, the colorfully pocketed ceiling reflects off the glimmering water, providing a stunning and refreshing reprieve from the heat of the day.

If you don't have any flotation devices with you, the pool is as far as you should go. However, if you have a small raft or PFD, walk through the swimming hole and toward the back you'll find a darkened passageway filled with water. Float down the liquid hallway and you'll quickly come across yet another small pool in this beautiful underground limestone palace. In the back swimming pool, some older children enjoy jumping from the small series of steps, but be sure the water is deep enough.

Bring a flotation device if you want to cruise down deep into the cave: It's worth it!

If it gets too chilly in the caves, there are also plenty of creekside spots to lounge in the sun.

FUN FACTOR: MOANING CAVERNS ADVENTURE PARK

If exploring the natural limestone caverns at Natural Bridges isn't enough for the adrenaline junkies in your family, head to the nearby Moaning Caverns Adventure Park. Just 5 minutes from the Natural Bridges Trailhead, Moaning Caverns is home to the largest single cave chamber in California and cave tours are available, along with spelunking. But underground exploration isn't all that is on the menu. Visitors can also pan for gold, practice their axe throwing, rock climb on the climbing wall, or zip along the park's zipline.

MILES AND DIRECTIONS

0.0 Find the trail by the round metal gate near the entrance to the parking area.

0.15 Trail junction; stay right on the forest road.

0.3 Pass a picnic table on the left side of the trail.

0.6 Trail junction; stay left.

0.7 Begin steeply descending down toward Coyote Creek.

1.0 You've reached the cave. When you're finished splashing, turn around and retrace your steps back to the parking area.

2.1 Arrive back at the parking area.

30 **NORTH GROVE TRAIL**

When you hike along the North Grove Trail, you're truly hiking into history. Historians consider the North Grove of sequoia trees to be the longest continuously operating tourist attraction in California since it was made known to non-Indigenous people in 1852. Today, the North Grove Trail is a family-friendly way to visit and admire the original leviathans.

Start: North Grove trailhead
Distance: 1.5-mile loop
Hiking time: About 2 hours
Difficulty: Easy
Elevation gain: 75 feet
Trail surface: Dirt
Hours open: 6 a.m. to 10 p.m.
Best season: Any season
Water: At the trailhead and in the visitor center
Toilets: At the trailhead
Nursing benches: Several benches along the trail
Stroller-friendly: Yes

Potential child hazards: None
Other trail users: None
Dogs: Not allowed
Land status: California Department of Parks and Recreation
Nearest town: Arnold
Fees and permits: Fee
Maps: Calaveras Big Trees State Park brochure
Trail contact: Calaveras Big Trees State Park, 1170 East CA 4, Arnold, CA 95223; (209) 795-2334; https://www.parks.ca.gov/?page_id=551
Gear suggestions: Sturdy shoes

FINDING THE TRAILHEAD

From Sacramento, take CA 99 south for approximately 28 miles. Take exit 271 toward Jahant Road. Turn left onto East Jahant Road / E Woodson Road and go approximately 9 miles. Turn right onto Mackville Road and drive 1.2 miles, and then turn left onto CA 12 east. Stay on CA 12 east for approximately 23 miles until it merges with CA 49 south. Stay on CA 49 for approximately 12 miles and then turn left onto CA 4 for 24 miles. Turn right into the State Park. There is a large parking lot at the visitor center where the trailhead begins. GPS: N38 16.95' / W120 17.75'

THE HIKE

Often, getting your kiddos to hit the trail involves a little bribery (or incentive, if we're being polite). For those days, consider heading toward the North Grove Trail. Not only does it have history, but when else can your children get to *literally* dance on top of a sequoia trunk–turned–dance stage?

In all seriousness, the story of how the stump came to be is quite tragic. A hunter named Augustus T. Dowd stumbled upon a "monstrous tree" in 1852 and ran back to town to tell all of his friends. No one believed his tall tales at first, but he eventually convinced a group of twenty people to follow a rough trail back to the magical tree (called the Discovery Tree) and witness its size for themselves.

News traveled fast. Almost immediately, visitors from all over the world were hiking up to see the Discovery Tree. But, its fame came with consequences. This was before sequoia trees had any protections in place. In 1853, a group of eager speculators stripped all the bark and felled the beautiful tree. It took five men 22 days of drilling holes with augers, and the tree still took many days to go down.

The stump of the famed Discovery Tree, both inspiring and heartbreaking

Tourist attractions ensued. The fallen tree was converted into a two-lane bowling alley and a bar while the stump itself was smoothed down and turned into a dance floor. While this did attract many visitors, it also came on the receiving end of wrath by famed naturalist John Muir, who was enraged at the desecration and commercialization of such a natural beauty.

Today, there is no bowling alley or bar, but the smoothed stump still lives alongside the North Grove Trail. While it is still a tourist attraction, we like to believe that this devastating story now acts as a lesson for all the families who witness the stump and are forced to only imagine what once was.

You can hop on the trail from a few different access points, but we began the hike at the Calaveras Big Trees State Park Visitor Center. The North Grove Trail is a loop that you can tackle in either direction. We recommend moving counterclockwise as the sign suggests.

Out of the gates, you'll encounter the stump of the Discovery Tree. It's tough to miss since there are often children playing or dancing on top of it. Regardless, this spectacle is a good way to start out for younger kids.

Almost immediately, the trail ambles through a large group of good-sized sequoias, all of them perfectly cylindrical as they reach toward the sky. While they aren't as large as some of the biggest ones, the noticeable grouping of reddish bark stands in nice contrast to a bluebird sky and is a good way to start the hike. These beauties continue for a few hundred yards, but the quantity tapers off around a quarter-mile.

The middle section of the trail is the quietest—meaning there aren't any famed trees to admire—and it's here that the light buzz of traffic from the nearby road begins to filter in. Press onward as the trail turns back toward the trailhead.

Standing beside one of the many
behemoths on the route

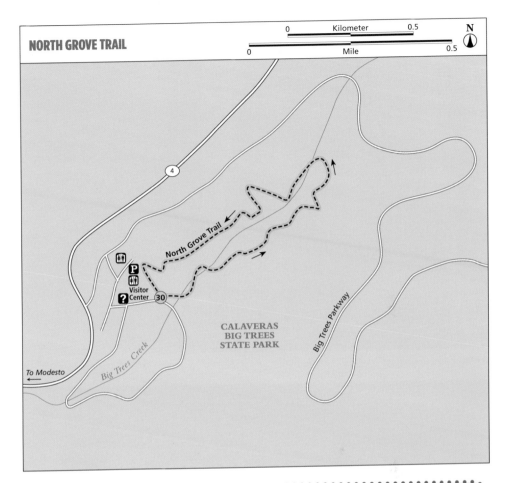

FUN FACTOR: TRANSPORT THE FAMILY BACK TO 1850

Just 20 minutes down the road in the small town of Murphy is the Murphy Historic Hotel, a unique opportunity to step back in time and live the way folks once did in the Wild West. The hotel first opened in the summer of 1856 and thrived since it was en route on the stagecoach to Big Tree Calaveras and the newfound giant trees. Famous guests like Mark Twain, President Ulysses S. Grant, and Thomas Lipton (the founder of Lipton Tea) stayed at the Murphy, and their original registration signatures are still on display in the hotel lobby.

Today, guests to the Murphy have two options for accommodations: twenty modernized and updated rooms or nine historic rooms that still reside in the original building above the saloon. These historic rooms are furnished with authentic furnishings from the era and do not have modern conveniences like television, telephones, or air-conditioning. All bathrooms are shared and in the hallway—just like in the 1850s.

Looking into the grove

The nearby creek is a perfect spot for a post-hike soak.

As you near the end of the loop, you'll come across the Pioneer Cabin Tree, one of the best-known sequoias in the country. Back in the 1950s when travel to these famed trees became a popular pastime, Calaveras found themselves in competition with Yosemite National Park since the roads into Yosemite Valley had improved. There in the park stood a tree called the Wawona Tunnel Tree, another massive sequoia that people had carved a tunnel through. People became enamored with the uniqueness of walking or driving a car through a tree, and the Wawona Tree grew famous. Feeling like they needed to keep up, the then-private owners of the North Grove did the same to the Pioneer Cabin Tree.

While the Wawona Tree eventually fell in 1969, the Pioneer Cabin Tree continued standing and even sprouting signs of new growth until 2017. But finally, a large rainstorm toppled the tree, so it's no longer possible to pass through the trunk. Still, hikers of the North Grove Trail can admire the tree on its side and marvel at its sheer size.

MILES AND DIRECTIONS

0.0   Begin at the Calaveras Big Trees Visitor Center and follow the signs that indicate counterclockwise direction. You'll see the stump from the Discovery Tree almost immediately.

0.2   A small spur trail jets to the right; stay straight. The right trail is the additional Grove Overlook trail.

0.3   Head north-northeast on the trail as it winds through the sequoia groves.

0.7   Trail intersection; stay left. The right trail is the Grove Overlook Trail looping back in.

0.8   The trail turns south back toward the trailhead.

1.3   The Pioneer Cabin Tree is highly visible on the trail.

1.5   You've closed the loop and returned to the trailhead.

31 PATRIARCH GROVE TRAIL

There are technically two hikes in this area. The shorter, quarter-mile hike along the commonly called Patriarch Grove Trail (aka Timberline Ancients) draws a crowd because it loops by the famous Patriarch Tree, one of the oldest living trees in the world and also one of the largest bristlecone pines. The Cottonwood Basin Trail is not much longer at only a half-mile, but it leads to a commanding overview that gives perspective to the edge of the Great Basin, a region that continues all the way to the Wasatch Range in Utah. Both trails depart from the same parking lot but head opposite directions, so you can make a figure-8 if you wish for a longer hike.

Start: Patriarch Grove trailhead
Distance: 0.4- to 0.8-mile loop
Hiking time: 30 minutes to 1 hour
Difficulty: Easy
Elevation gain: 80 to 120 feet
Trail surface: Dirt and rock
Hours open: 6 a.m. to 10 p.m.
Best season: Spring to autumn
Water: At the Ancient Bristlecone Pine Forest Visitor Center
Toilets: At the trailhead
Nursing benches: None
Stroller-friendly: No
Potential child hazards: None
Other trail users: None

Dogs: Allowed on leash
Land status: US Forest Service
Nearest town: Lone Pine
Fees and permits: Fee per person with max per car, but kids under 18 free
Maps: Inyo National Forest, Patriarch Grove area map
Trail contact: Inyo National Forest, 351 Pacu Ln., Ste. 200, Bishop, CA 93514; (760) 873-2400; www.fs.usda.gov/inyo
Gear suggestions: Sturdy shoes and sunscreen (there is little to no shade)

FINDING THE TRAILHEAD

From Bakersfield, take CA 58 east for approximately 55 miles. Take exit 167 to CA 14 toward Bishop/Mojave and go 46 miles. Continue onto US 395 north for 107 miles and then turn right onto CA 168 east for approximately 13 miles. Turn left onto White Mountain Road for the next 10 miles until you reach the Ancient Bristlecone Pine Forest Visitor Center (you'll know it when you reach the end of the paved road). Make sure to fill up on water and use the toilet since there is nothing at the trailhead. Continue on the dirt road for another 12 miles. At the fork, stay right toward Patriarch Grove trailhead for another mile when you reach the end of the road. The dirt road is not recommended for light passenger vehicles with no four-wheel drive or all-wheel drive. Parking is limited. GPS: N37 31.63' / W118 11.87'

THE HIKE

The drive to the trailhead is half the fun . . . but make sure you have the right vehicle to do it. We've seen standard sedans at the trailhead, and with some thoughtful driving it's entirely possible, but it will be a lot easier if you have a higher clearance vehicle (stock is fine) to dodge some of the rocks on the 13-mile dirt road. Fortunately the scenery is splendid because you're driving near treeline, and the time passes fairly quickly even when driving slowly.

Detail of the gnarled growth

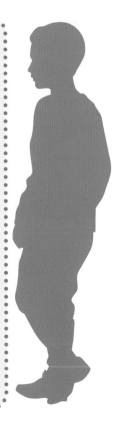

FUN FACTOR: CLIMB ONE OF THE HIGHEST PEAKS IN CALIFORNIA

If you're a peakbagging family, you've already driven much of the way to the trailhead for one of California's more unusual Fourteeners: White Mountain. A Fourteener is any peak that crests 14,000 feet in elevation (Mount Whitney is the tallest in the continental United States at 14,495 feet), and California has twelve of them. White Mountain is unusual because of its approach and surrounding terrain. Since you're above treeline almost the entire way, the views are absolutely spectacular, but you also have a good sense of just how far you have to go from the moment you leave the trailhead. The 7-mile approach gains 3,300 feet while mostly following a four-wheel-drive road, so navigation is pretty straightforward. Don't be fooled by the simplicity: You'll need plenty of water for your hike, and at this elevation the weather can get harsh and cold in a hurry. Also, altitude sickness can quickly ruin a trip (especially when coming from sea level), so be sure to hydrate well before, during, and after your hike. Once you get behind on hydration, it is hard to make it up, so if you feel early symptoms of altitude sickness, you should turn around right away. Also: We highly recommend going slower than you feel is necessary, especially at the start. Let your body settle in, keep a close eye on the rest of your family, and remember that getting to the top is optional; getting back down is mandatory.

Looking back toward the parking lot as the trail heads to the overlook

One of the many beautiful trailside specimens

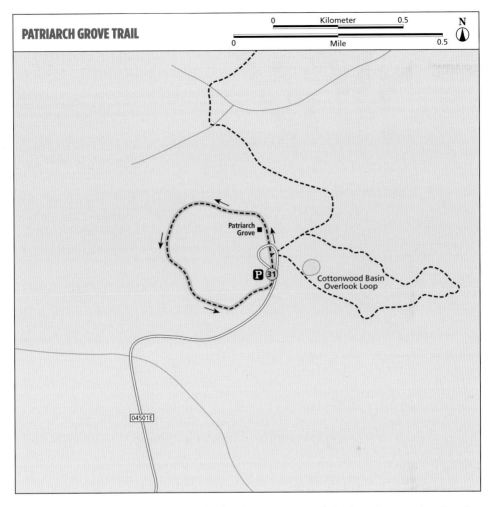

Once at the parking lot, start by heading west toward the large interpretive sign that gives an overview of the area. Continue on the trail in a counterclockwise direction (assuming you want to see the Patriarch Grove ASAP) and marvel at being in the presence of the oldest nonclonal tree on the planet.

And when we say old, we mean *old*. These trees have seen the Egyptian Empire, Roman Empire, the Middle Ages, the Renaissance, and all of modern history. Some of the oldest are celebrating their 5,000th+ birthday! It's fitting the exposed, wind-whipped terrain shapes these trees into gnarled shapes—the growth pattern is called krummholz— as they look like they've borne the weight of time on their shoulders for millennia. These distinct shapes also make them famous for photography, and because there is little to obstruct early or evening sun, the golden hour light is particularly special. Bonus: If you time it right, you can hike sans headlamp under a full moon, when the landscape really takes on a lunar feel.

Option: After you complete the loop (which takes anywhere from 30 minutes to 2 hours, depending on how many rocks your kids try to put in their pockets), cross to the other side of the lot and head out to the Cottonwood Basin Overlook. This has similar

Looking west across the valley at sunset

features to the Timberline Ancients trail, but it's about double the length with a bit more steepness as well. Once you get to the view, you'll get a good sense of how desolate your immediate surroundings are relative to lower in the valley below, which underscores how impressive it is the bristlecone pines have survived as long as they have. Once you've had your fill, continue on the trail where it quickly does a hairpin turn and heads back to the parking lot.

MILES AND DIRECTIONS

0.0 From the parking area, turn left and begin the loop in a counterclockwise direction.

0.1 Almost immediately, spot the placard for the Patriarch Tree.

0.4 Return to the beginning and close the loop.

32 SONOMA OVERLOOK TRAIL

Steeped in history and ecology, the Sonoma Overlook Trail resides on what was once a scruffy and abandoned hillside perched above the small community of Sonoma. Today, it's a 2.5-mile walking path filled with wine-country views and native plants and wildlife at every turn. Sections can be steep for young children, so the Upper Trailhead is a good alternative that cuts off a large chunk of the climb.

Start: Sonoma Overlook trailhead
Distance: 2.5-mile lollipop loop
Hiking time: About 2 hours
Difficulty: Easy
Elevation gain: 380 feet
Trail surface: Dirt
Hours open: Dawn to dusk
Best season: Spring to autumn (lower portion of Sonoma Overlook trail is closed in the winter)
Water: None
Toilets: None
Nursing benches: None
Stroller-friendly: No

Potential child hazards: Poison ivy
Other trail users: None
Dogs: Not allowed
Land status: County Preserve
Nearest town: Sonoma
Fees and permits: None
Maps: Sonoma Overlook and Montini Preserve trails map
Trail contact: Sonoma Ecology Center, 15000 Arnold Dr. Creekside Complex, Sonoma, CA 95431; (707) 996-0712; sonomaecologycenter.org/sonoma-overlook-trail
Gear suggestions: Sturdy shoes

FINDING THE TRAILHEAD

From San Francisco, take US 101 north for approximately 22 miles. Take exit 460A to CA 37 east toward Napa/Vallejo and go 7 miles. Turn left onto CA 121 north for 7.5 miles and then turn left onto CA 12 west. Stay on CA 12 for 3.7 miles and then turn left onto West Napa Street and then an immediate right onto 1st Street West for a half-mile. Look for signs for Mountain Cemetery and park in the first parking lot on your left. GPS: N38 17.98' / W122 27.43'

THE HIKE

With its proximity to town, the Sonoma Overlook Trail is a local favorite, and it's not uncommon to spot hikers and trail runners who clearly navigate this route every week. But even if you're not from the area, the hike is a good one if only to learn that there is more to Sonoma than wine.

Because the Sonoma Overlook Trail is so beloved by the community, it is a well-trodden path that is easy to follow and clearly marked. In fact, there are even self-guided checklists in the kiosks at the trailhead for hikers wanting to learn more about the trees, wildflowers, and birds along the way. If you can time it right and visit the area in spring or early summer, the lower meadows are dotted with an explosion of colorful wildflowers like milkmaids, buttercups, lupines, and California fuchsia.

Begin the 2.5-mile out-and-back at the parking area (although some opt to begin near the cemetery to the east of the trailhead). Hike uphill, gaining a moderate elevation almost immediately. Thanks to the dense vegetation, there is a lot of shade on the trail which is nice during warm summer afternoons, but keep an eye on your feet. With quite a few rocks in the trail, it's easy to misstep.

The well-signed start of the trail

As you continue in elevation, the dirt trail winds through grassy, shaded spaces.

The start of the hike is well maintained with beautiful rockwork like this.

Still, the lower section of the trail is a delight as it wraps through a series of mixed evergreens alongside a dominant display of bay and coast live oak. A variety of oak are also native to the trail and species like black oak, Oregon oak, and blue oak are mixed into woodlands along the path. Pro tip: Everybody's favorite poison oak is also common on the Sonoma Overlook Trail and can be found frequently as you ascend. Be sure to warn your kiddos to stay on the trail and not touch any of the plants.

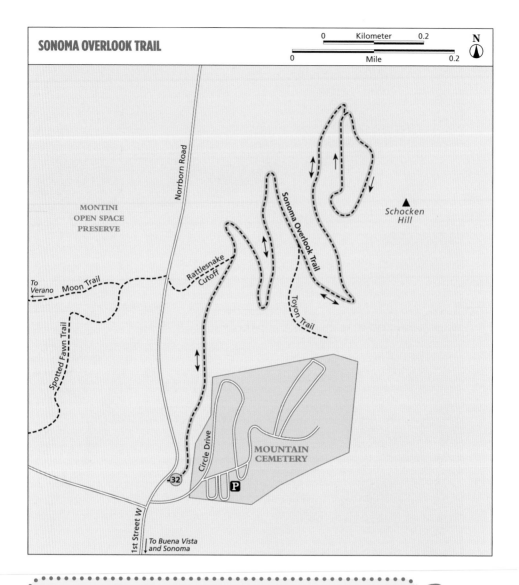

0   Kilometer   0.2

0   Mile   0.2

N

MONTINI
OPEN SPACE
PRESERVE

Norborn Road

Sonoma Overlook Trail

Schocken
Hill

To
Verano   Moon Trail

Rattlesnake
Cutoff

Toyon Trail

Spotted Fawn Trail

Circle Drive

MOUNTAIN
CEMETERY

32

P

1st Street W

To Buena Vista
and Sonoma

FUN FACTOR: CATCH A TRAIN AT THE RAILYARD

Sonoma has quite a few options for families, but the Sonoma TrainTown Railroad is one of our favorites. TrainTown boasts a quarter-scale railroad with 4 miles of actual track that amounts to a 20-minute train ride for kids of all ages. The train goes through tunnels, over bridges, and even stops at the facility's own petting zoo. But that's not all TrainTown has to lure your children into a day of fun! In addition to the train ride, train-themed rides are available. There is a carousel, a Ferris wheel, and even a mine train mini-coaster.

Once you're done, head back to Sonoma where you'll find plenty of family-friendly dining stretched around town. Good options include Mary's Pizza Shack, The Red Grape, and of course, Sweet Scoops Homemade Ice Cream.

One of the many overlooks across the Sonoma region

Continue uphill, gaining roughly 125 feet in the first quarter-mile. The trail turns right at a third of a mile, beginning a small series of switchbacks. You'll work through two pairs of these switchbacks when you see a small trail on the right side at 0.7 mile. This is the Toyon Trail, a quarter-mile spur trail that heads back to the Upper Trailhead, the alternative place to begin if you want to cut some distance off your hike.

Work through one more switchback that steadily climbs the last section of trail before arriving at the high point of 535 feet, nearly 450 feet higher than where you began. Here, stay left to tackle the small loop (it's a third-mile around the entire section) in a clockwise direction. This loop is known as the Upper Loop Trail, and you can easily cut it off the hike if you want to shorten the distance.

Close the loop and head back down the trail, retracing your steps back to the parking lot.

MILES AND DIRECTIONS

0.0   Start on the dirt path to the north of the parking lot, just behind the trail sign.

0.1   Pass through a series of dense vegetation that comes and goes as you ascend.

0.3   View a small trail to the left as it angles back downhill. This is Rattlesnake Cutoff, a trail that heads southwest back toward town.

0.35 You're reached your first in a series of switchbacks as the trail turns right.

0.7   The Toyon Trail descends down to the right, heading back to the Upper Trailhead. Stay left.

1.1   Reach the top of the climb and arrive at the beginning of the Upper Loop Trail. Stay left and complete the loop in a clockwise direction.

1.4   Close the loop and turn left. Retrace your steps back to the car.

2.5   Arrive back at the car.

33 SOUTH TUFA TRAIL

The tufa formations are natural works of art and possibly something you've never seen before. Combined with the unusual setting of Mono Lake, this entire hike is like walking through a science museum. The hike itself is extremely mellow, but even though it's a short distance you should plan on spending more time here than you think.

Start: South Tufa trailhead
Distance: 0.8-mile loop
Hiking time: About 1 hour
Difficulty: Easy
Elevation gain: 40 feet
Trail surface: Dirt and rock
Hours open: Dawn to dusk
Best season: Any season
Water: At the Mono Lake Scenic Area Visitor Center
Toilets: At the trailhead
Nursing benches: None
Stroller-friendly: No
Potential child hazards: None

Other trail users: None
Dogs: Allowed on leash
Land status: California Department of Parks and Recreation
Nearest town: Lee Vining
Fees and permits: Fee per person
Maps: Mono Lake Tufa State Natural Reserve park brochure
Trail contact: Mono Lake Tufa State Natural Reserve, US 395, Lee Vining, CA 93541; (760) 647-6331; www .parks.ca.gov/?page_id=514
Gear suggestions: Sturdy shoes

FINDING THE TRAILHEAD

From Modesto, take CA 108 east for approximately 31 miles until you merge onto CA 120 east. Stay on CA 120 east for 62 miles, turn right onto US 395 south/CA 120 east, and go for approximately 5 miles. Take a left to stay on CA 120 east for another 5 miles. Turn left to head toward Test Station Road for 1 mile. The road ends at the trailhead. There is plenty of parking. GPS: N37 56.32' / W119 1.62'

THE HIKE

Start from the parking lot on the southern side of Mono Lake and head north on the boardwalk for about a third of a mile. You can clearly see the formations from the start of your hike, and the visual context is a nice complement to the experience once you get up close to the tufa.

The tufa formations result from subsurface calcium-rich freshwater springs reacting with the high levels of carbonate in the water. This produces limestone near the underwater spring, and over the course of centuries these towers can grow upwards of 30 feet underwater. These formations used to be wholly or partially submerged, but the receding lake levels provide a fuller view of the unusual tower structures. Ask your kids what shape the formations remind them of; like finding shapes in clouds, we've found the level of maturity of your children can result in a variety of answers.

At the end of the boardwalk the trail turns to sand, and you make your way in a clockwise fashion from interpretive sign to interpretive sign. Our daughter mostly played on the beach and chased the swarms of alkali flies, which are one of the foundations of the food chain here. The water here has extremely high levels of salinity (much more than the Pacific), but it still supports organisms like the Mono Lake brine shrimp that support the migratory bird populations.

Follow the boardwalk north to the beach with the tufa formations.

Once you hit the beach, look for signs like this one to follow through the formations.

Some of the larger formations

Once you hit the beach, the trail wends through the formations in a clockwise fashion, with some social trails making it less obvious as to which one will return you to the boardwalk. No matter; the distinct formations make navigation easy, and if you're forced to retrace your steps, you'll get a good look at the tufa with the Sierra Crest in the background.

As you start to head back toward the trailhead, there is also an informal trail that leads to Navy Beach. This is another good play area for kids that only adds about 0.6 mile to your hike and reveals beautiful views of the South Tufa formations to boot. If you've arrived near sunset and you're waiting for the right light, this is a great way to pass the time with the family.

A final note: This area has a sordid history when it comes to California's water wars. It's worth doing significantly more research on the subject than will fit in this text, but

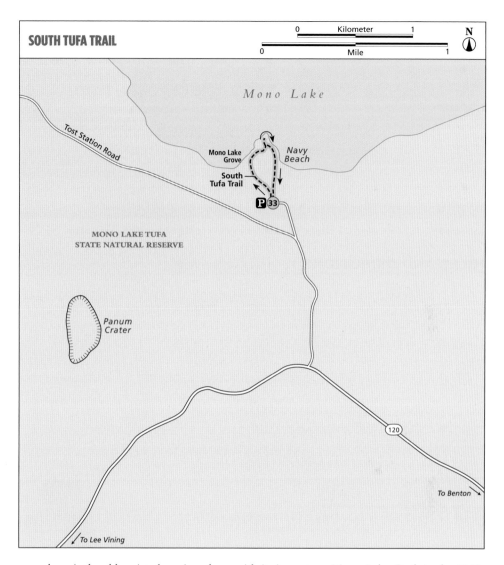

Mono Lake

Tost Station Road

Mono Lake
Grove

Navy
Beach

South
Tufa Trail

P 33

MONO LAKE TUFA
STATE NATURAL RESERVE

Panum
Crater

120

To Benton

To Lee Vining

here is the abbreviated version along with its impact on Mono Lake. Back in the 1940s the Los Angeles Department of Water and Power (LADWP) had already drained Owens Lake just south of here, so they extended the aqueduct system to Mono Lake. Forty years later the water levels dropped low enough that a land bridge formed between the end of the lake and the island in the middle where migratory birds had safely nested for generations. Now predators could safely make it to the island, which decimated the bird population and affected the local ecosystem in a material way. After about a decade of tangling in court, the California State Water Resources ordered protection for the lake and set a target of holding the waterline at 6,392 feet. This effort successfully submerged the land bridge again, although we're still not quite back at the prescribed levels. Interestingly this South Tufa trail would not exist without the lower water levels, so in some ways you could say this hike may one day disappear if we achieve our goals of higher water conservation.

Look for the alkali flies along the beach; these are one of the cornerstones of the ecosystem.

MILES AND DIRECTIONS

0.0   From the parking area to the west of the restrooms, find the path that heads north toward Mono Lake.

0.1   Trail split; turn left to complete the loop in a clockwise direction.

0.2   Arrive at the South Tufa Grove.

0.4   Beautiful overlook of Mono Lake.

0.5   Turn south and begin heading back toward the parking area.

0.6   Trail junction; stay right. If you go left, you will also return to the same parking area, only with a slightly longer distance beneath your feet.

0.8   You've arrived back at the parking area.

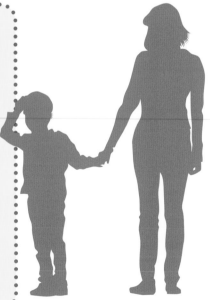

FUN FACTOR: WATER PLAY ON THE LAKE

If your kids are responsible with water safety, we highly recommend renting a stand-up paddleboard or kayak and touring the lake. One of the highlights is paddling out from Navy Beach (referenced in this chapter) since it is one of the easiest spots to launch watercraft. We recommend heading out in the morning while the lake is relatively smooth; there are regular winds that whip the lake surface in the afternoon and can make it genuinely difficult to safely return to your harbor. Stay close to the shoreline as there is plenty to see without getting into the middle of the lake if you don't have the experience. For those who do have extensive experience, one of the highlights is paddling out to Paoha Island for a picnic. Make sure to check in with the visitor center to ensure you aren't in conflict with the annual closure for nesting birds, and you'll also need a permit to be out on the water.

34 TRAIL OF THE GARGOYLES: SOUTH RIM

Stunning geology, commanding views, and enough occasional exposure to please the feistiest of kiddos make Trail of the Gargoyles a crowd favorite among families. The distance is manageable for the smallest of legs too, so even young kids can enjoy time on the trail. Just be aware of the steep dropoffs!

Start: Trail of the Gargoyles trailhead
Distance: 1.0-mile out-and-back
Hiking time: About 1 hour
Difficulty: Easy
Elevation gain: 100 feet
Trail surface: Dirt and rock
Hours open: Dawn to dusk
Best season: Late spring to early winter
Water: None
Toilets: None
Nursing benches: None
Stroller-friendly: No

Potential child hazards: Steep dropoffs
Other trail users: None
Dogs: Allowed on leash
Land status: US Forest Service
Nearest town: Pinecrest
Fees and permits: None
Maps: Stanislaus National Forest map
Trail contact: Summit Ranger District, 1 Pinecrest Lake Rd., Pinecrest, CA 95364; (209) 965-3434; www.fs.usda.gov/stanislaus
Gear suggestions: Sturdy shoes

FINDING THE TRAILHEAD

From Modesto, take CA 108 east for approximately 71 miles. Then turn right onto FR 4N12 and then stay left at the fork. At the second fork, bear right and at the third fork, bear left. You'll be on FR 4N12 for a total of 6.7 miles. Turn left onto FSR 18EV529 and end at the Trail of the Gargoyles trailhead. Parking is limited but usually not very busy. GPS: N38 14.95' / W119 56.59'

THE HIKE

Sometimes we need our kids to holler, "Hey, that's really cool!" to feel validated in our choices. Trail of the Gargoyles is one trail that will make you feel like you picked a good one for your family. Added bonus: If your children are fans of Disney's *Frozen* or *Hunchback of Notre Dame* movies, they're likely to enjoy the rock formations at the end; they look oddly similar to the rock characters in either film!

The trail itself begins in the parking lot before heading due west and approaching the canyon rim. Very quickly, it will sharply turn left. (The route to the right is the North Rim, a 1.5-mile option that views the rock formations from a different angle. If your family has extra energy, consider tackling both hikes during the day!) Now, you're hiking along the rim of the canyon and will continue to do so for the entire hike. Pro tip: Stay away from the edge and be sure to remind your children of the same. It's very possible that the crumbling edge of the canyon would give way beneath your feet.

As you're trekking along the rim, you'll notice a few numbered stops. These correlate with an information guide that details the background behind many of the formations. If you'd like to learn more, snag a guide at the Summit Ranger District Office or at the trailhead (when available).

Follow the cliffside trail as it wraps around the edge of the canyon.

One of the more textured rock formations you'll see along the trail's edge

Some of the eponymous gargoyles

Depending on when you hike, the classic Sierra wildflowers along the trail are worthy of a visit on their own. In late spring or early summer, a dazzling mix of lupine, phlox, mule's ears, and paintbrush flowers speckle the surrounding area, coloring the horizon with a cheerful mix of reds and purples and yellows.

If you can't make it for wildflower season, don't sweat it: There is plenty of good stuff to see. As you stroll down the moderately flat path (there is only 100 feet of elevation

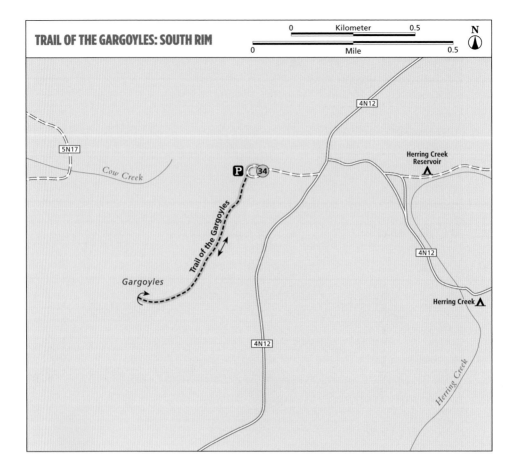

0   Kilometer   0.5

0   Mile   0.5

N

4N12

5N17

Cow Creek

Herring Creek Reservoir

P 34

Trail of the Gargoyles

4N12

Gargoyles

Herring Creek

4N12

Herring Creek

Looking back toward the trailhead (a little left of center) at sunset

gain), you'll notice a myriad of strange rock formations filling the cliff bands along the canyon rim. These gargoyle-like shapes are thanks to a number of historical volcanic events including lava flows, ash deposits, and volcanic mudflows.

Continue hiking up the trail, cresting the "high point" at 0.4 mile. Once you're here, you're done with the barely noticeable climb—and you've almost reached the end. Hike 0.1 mile farther and you'll arrive at the destination: the final viewpoint.

From here, you can glimpse a panoramic view of the canyon, along with a number of the bizarre gargoyle formations filling your eyesight. Spend a little time here, admiring the work of Mother Nature. When you're ready, turn around and retrace your steps back to the trailhead.

MILES AND DIRECTIONS

0.0 From the parking area, find the path that leaves from the south side of the lot.

0.4 You've reached the trail's high point.

0.5 Arrive at the Trail of the Gargoyles overlook. Turn around and retrace your steps back to the trailhead.

1.0 Arrive back at the trailhead.

35 UPPER KINNEY LAKE VIA THE PACIFIC CREST TRAIL

Located on Ebbetts Pass off the northbound route of the Pacific Crest Trail, Upper Kinney Lake gives families a lot of bang for their buck: high-alpine scenery with minimal physical output. Save for the initial climb, this hike is a mellow tromp through wildflower-speckled meadows and trout-filled sparkling waters.

Start: Pacific Crest trailhead
Distance: 4.1-mile lollipop loop
Hiking time: About 5 hours
Difficulty: Moderate
Elevation gain: 630 feet
Trail surface: Dirt and rock
Hours open: Dawn to dusk (the road to the trailhead closes in the winter)
Best season: Late spring to early autumn
Water: None
Toilets: None
Nursing benches: None
Stroller-friendly: No

Potential child hazards: None
Other trail users: None
Dogs: Allowed on leash
Land status: US Forest Service
Nearest town: Bear Valley
Fees and permits: None
Maps: Humboldt-Toiyabe National Forest map
Trail contact: Humboldt-Toiyabe National Forest Bridgeport Ranger District, HC62 Box 1000, Bridgeport, CA 93517; (760) 932-7070; www.fs .usda.gov/htnf
Gear suggestions: Sturdy shoes

FINDING THE TRAILHEAD

From Stockton, take CA 4 east for approximately 114 miles. There is a small pullout with room for about ten cars at Ebbetts Pass. The trailhead starts about 100 yards east of the pass along the PCT. GPS: N38 32.81' / W119 48.64'

THE HIKE

Admittedly, we found this trail by accident. When driving up Ebbetts Pass to locate Ebbetts Peak (another chapter in this book), we zipped by a small cluster of hikers standing on the side of CA 4.

We didn't know why they were there or what was happening, but it piqued our interest. After hiking Ebbetts Peak, we returned to the group and realized it was a designated stop for "Trail Magic" (see sidebar). As one of many waypoints along the 2,653-mile Pacific Crest Trail (PCT), a group of Good Samaritans had set up a table with juice and homemade snacks to hand out to weary hikers working their way north to the Canadian border.

We loved the idea and also became interested in the hike itself. While we definitely were not going to hike the PCT that day, a few chatty adventurers told us about Kinney Lakes that were just a few miles away. Looking to bask in the warm summer day, we loaded our daughter into the kid carrier and tackled our abbreviated version of the PCT.

From the highway, the trail immediately ascends in a daunting fashion, but don't stress. Albeit slightly strenuous, this first climb covers the majority of the elevation gain on the hike. You'll tackle nearly 200 feet in the first quarter-mile, but after that the trail levels out to a leisurely stroll.

If you have time to stop by Lake Alpine after the hike, your kids will thank you.

FUN FACTOR: MAKE A LITTLE MAGIC

Thru-hikers like those trekking the Pacific Crest Trail are often traveling for months and months at a time without any comfort of home. They sleep in their tents for the entire summer, and only eat food that they can carry in their backpacks. For this reason, the concept of "Trail Magic" has been on the rise in recent years, and it can be a fun day of citizenship to enjoy with your kids. However, there are a few things to keep in mind if you decide to set up a Trail Magic station.

- Always follow Leave No Trace principles. Don't carry anything onto the trail that you can't clean up and take back out with you.
- Personally manage the Trail Magic station rather than leaving the treats unattended. Many well-wishers think that leaving treats out there will serve more hikers, but animals often get into the treats and rip things to shreds. Not only does this leave a lot of trash on the trail, but it's also bad for the animals' health.
- Remember that trail magic doesn't have to be food or beverages. There are many comforts that thru-hikers yearn for on their journeys such as free rides into town to replenish their supplies or opening your home for an afternoon to offer up a hot shower. Once, we saw a thru-hiker in a store looking for a new sun hat since hers had been ruined. We overheard her expressing concern to her friend about the price, so we paid for it when we checked out with our hiking supplies. We left and never told her, but we like to imagine the joy she experienced upon learning her sun hat was gifted to her!

Fresh trailside dew and lupine

Once the initial hill is accomplished, the trail turns sharply toward the northwest and wraps through a series of alpine meadows. Late in the summer, the tall verdant grass blows lightly in the breeze, but we recommend visiting in early summer or late spring, if possible. When timed just right, this trail arguably boasts some of the best wildflower viewing in the area. Thanks to the cooler nights at high altitudes, the peak bloom occurs later than at lower elevations, so early to mid-June typically secures spectacular vistas

Hip-high summertime bloom can make anyone cheery on the trail.

Enjoying a mama-daughter picnic beside the lake

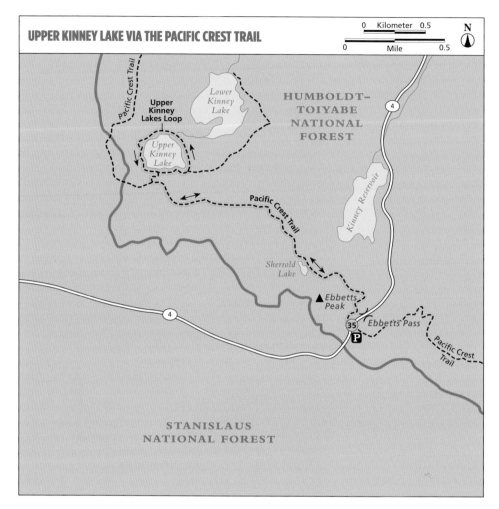

filled with corn lilies and penstemon in the foreground and snowcapped mountains in the background.

At 0.5, the trail splits. Stay to the right and skirt between two smaller bodies of water: This is Sherrold Lake and it is a popular campsite for thru-hikers on the PCT.

Continue onward, as the trail gently undulates through lightly treed meadows. To your right, you'll catch a glimpse of a large lake down the slope. This is Kinney Reservoir, not to be confused with the Upper or Lower Kinney Lake that you're hiking toward. It's a popular spot for anglers looking to snag rainbow trout as it's easily accessible from the highway.

Around 1.0 mile, you'll feel the trail turn due west for almost a half-mile before it wraps back toward the north. Once you make this turn, you'll know that you've almost arrived at the lake. From here, it's all downhill to Upper Kinney Lake.

At 1.7 miles, the lake will come into view. If you want to picnic or swim in the water, split right and descend toward Upper Kinney as the PCT continues wrapping to the west and away from the lake. The west side of the lake is a popular campsite for thru-hikers, but you can easily nab solitude by hiking to the east side of the lake where it's relatively quiet. From here, you can also score views of the lesser-visited Lower Kinney Lake that sits 200 feet below.

When you're ready to turn around, retrace your steps back the way you came. On the return, take a look to the right as you pass by Sherrold Lake. Just a few miles away sits Ebbetts Peak, the quick peakbagging route from Hike 24. If you're hiking with older kids or your family simply has lots of energy, these two hikes are a good duo to pair together for a single-day adventure.

MILES AND DIRECTIONS

0.0   If you park at the pass, the trailhead can be tricky to spot. Walk about 100 yards down CA 4 to the noticeable locations where the PCT crosses the road. From here, you'll easily spot the trail.

0.5   A small trail spurs off to the right; this route goes back to Ebbetts Pass. Stay straight to head toward Upper Kinney Lake.

1.6   Trail junction; stay right at the marked sign to head down to Upper Kinney Lake. The Pacific Crest Trail continues on toward the left.

1.7   The trail splits as it wraps around Upper Kinney Lake. From here, hike in whichever direction to circumnavigate the lake, enjoying a picnic at the best site you can find.

2.4   Close the loop around the lake and retrace your steps back to the car.

4.1   Arrive back at the parking area.

36 WOLF HOUSE HISTORIC TRAIL

Budding adventurers and literary buffs alike will appreciate the history and family-friendly trails offered at Jack London State Historic Park. Situated on land that was once part of Beauty Ranch and owned by renowned writer Jack London, the Wolf House Historic Trail takes hikers on a walk through time to view the ruins of London's one-day forever home.

Start: Wolf House trailhead
Distance: 1.5-mile out-and-back
Hiking time: About 1 hour
Difficulty: Easy
Elevation gain: 259 feet
Trail surface: Dirt and pavement
Hours open: 9 a.m. to 5 p.m.
Best season: Any season
Water: Drinking fountains at the visitor center, gravesite, and Wolf House
Toilets: At the parking lot, gravesite, and Wolf House
Nursing benches: Picnic tables at the parking lot and Wolf House
Stroller-friendly: Yes

Potential child hazards: None
Other trail users: None
Dogs: Allowed on leash
Land status: California Department of Parks and Recreation
Nearest town: Kenwood
Fees and permits: Day-use fee
Maps: Jack London State Historic Park brochure
Trail contact: Jack London State Historic Park, 2400 London Ranch Rd., Glen Ellen, CA 95442; (707) 938-5216; www.parks.ca.gov/?page_id=478
Gear suggestions: Sturdy shoes

FINDING THE TRAILHEAD

From Sacramento, take I-80 south for approximately 46 miles and take exit 39B for CA 12 west toward Napa/Sonoma. Travel for approximately 15 miles and make a slight right onto Napa Road and go 6.2 miles. Take a right at the end of the road onto Arnold Drive and continue for 3.6 miles. At the traffic circle, continue straight to stay on Arnold Drive for another 3.3 miles. Turn left onto London Ranch Road and into the State Historic Park. Parking is at the Wolf Lodge lower lot and the trailhead is on the eastern side. GPS: N38 21.38' / W122 32.49'

THE HIKE

Most book lovers know Jack London from his 1903 masterpiece, *The Call of the Wild*. The adventure novel chronicles the life of a sled dog named Buck in Yukon, Canada, who lives during the 1890s Klondike gold rush era. But, *The Call of the Wild* was just one of many instances when London wrote about dogs or wolves. In fact, his friend George Sterling gave him the nickname "The Wolf" since London so often touched on the topic.

So, when London and his wife, Charmian, began construction on their dream home in 1911, it was appropriate that it be named the Wolf House.

Designed by San Francisco architect Albert L. Farr, Wolf House meant to boast 15,000 square feet spread over twenty-six rooms, nine fireplaces, and a two-story-high living room. Aware of the catastrophic 1906 earthquake that destroyed more than 80 percent of San Francisco, London and Farr worked to create a fantastically strong and durable home.

Running from shady spot to shady spot

Yes, our daughter literally skips on the trail.

FUN FACTOR: EXPLORE THE PARK

While Wolf House is a main attraction in Jack London Historic Park, it isn't the only activity to engage your kiddos. In particular, children of all ages will get a kick out of the Pig Palace, a historic housing system for all of London's pigs. Built in 1915, it allowed a single individual to care for 200 pigs on his own. A central two-story tower drops feet below while seventeen hog troughs—each with its own courtyard, food and water troughs, fenced outdoor run, and covered sleeping area—surround the structure. Kids are often enamored with the elaborate housing facility since it is quite nice, even by today's standards. In fact, it earned its nickname the Pig Palace when a local newspaper reporter learned of the $3,000 price tag to construct the fortunate pigs' homes.

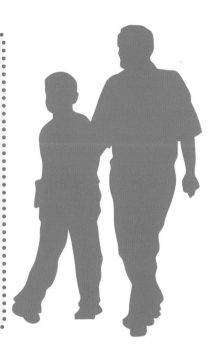

The subject of this trail's name

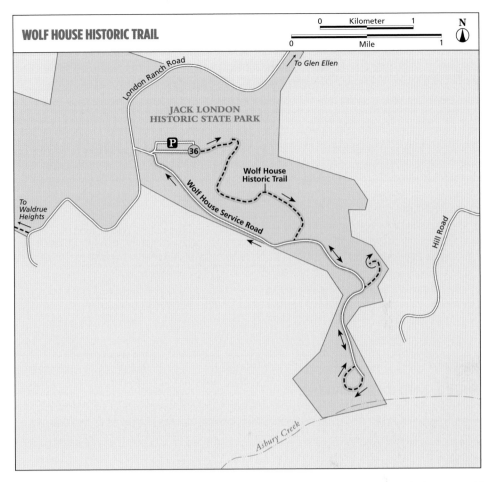

JACK LONDON
HISTORIC STATE PARK

Wolf House
Historic Trail

Wolf House Service Road

London Ranch Road

To Glen Ellen

To
Waldrue
Heights

Hill Road

Asbury Creek

However, London and Charmian never got the opportunity to actually live in Wolf House. The house was almost done when a late-night fire broke out on August 22, 1913. It quickly spread throughout the home, completely demolishing the interior. By morning, only the thick stone walls remained. Arson was suspected at the time, but today's experts now believe that the fire began due to spontaneous combustion from linseed oil–soaked rags left behind by workers.

Regardless, London never called Wolf House his home, but thanks to the durable construction, the building still stands today for hikers to visit.

Begin hiking at the House of Happy Walls museum, after leaving your car in the nearby parking lot. The museum itself makes for a great visit before or after the hike, especially for history enthusiasts. After London's death in 1916, Charmian and London's stepsister, Eliza Shepard, built the House of Happy Walls. Charmian constructed the building with explicit wishes in mind when she said, "it is not to be lived in by anyone except a caretaker. This building and its arrangements are peculiarly an expression of myself and its ultimate purpose is that of a museum to Jack London and myself."

Assuming you tour House of Happy Walls before your hike, exit the museum on the paved walkway and take the trail to the left of the entrance. Almost immediately, you'll see a large sign on your left as a trail descends a small hill. This is the official start to the Wolf House Historic Trail.

At 0.3 mile, the trail breaks free from the forest and drops you into an open meadow. If you time it right and visit during the spring bloom, this meadow is a veritable cornucopia of wildflowers in a variety of colors. If not, it's still a wonderful spot for bird-watching and makes for a great change of pace on the trail.

Continue hiking for another 0.1 mile and you will arrive at a trail junction with the service road. Stay to the left. (If you take a right, you'll return to the beginning; this is the return route.) After another mellow 0.1 mile, you and the kiddos will again reach a second trail junction. If you opt to take a left, you can hike a 0.1-mile spur dirt trail that goes to the Jack London gravesite. This is well worth a visit as both London and Charmian are buried on a knoll overlooking the Valley of the Moon. (This is included in the overall mileage.)

Veer right at the second junction and stay on the paved path. Almost immediately, the trail severely dips down, losing more than 130 feet of elevation in a tenth of a mile. Once you hit the low point, you've arrived at Wolf House.

Free, docent-guided tours of Wolf House are available on weekends. But, if you visit at other times, there is often a guide set up at a table, happy and willing to answer any questions or provide any historical context. Visitors may wander around the perimeter, or venture inside via the staircase and contained space that was reconstructed for guests.

Once you're done perusing the ruins, return the way you came. When you reach the trail junction at 1.2 miles, stay left and return to the beginning via the service road.

MILES AND DIRECTIONS

0.0 Begin hiking on the paved trail that leaves from the east side of the Lower Parking Lot.

0.1 Pass Happy Walls House Museum on the left side.

0.3 Break free from the dense trees into a small meadow that fills with wildflowers in the spring.

0.4 Trail junction; turn left. You're now hiking on the service road that will take you back to the parking lot upon your return.

0.5 Trail junction; to your left is the short spur trail to Jack London's gravesite. Once you're done exploring the area, stay left to continue onto the Wolf Historic House.

0.8 You've arrived at the Wolf Historic House. Loop around the perimeter to explore. When you're finished, begin retracing your steps back to the car.

1.2 Trail junction; stay straight to remain on the service road that takes you back to the parking area.

1.5 Arrive back at the parking area.

37 YOST CREEK TRAIL: FIRE STATION TO SKI AREA

This trail starts in town and feels like it practically runs straight up the hill, so we don't recommend it for children who are still finding their hiking legs. But for parents with kid carriers or older kids who are looking to prove their strength, you quickly get to great views of June Lake and the local town, and the top out at June Meadows Chalet is the perfect spot for a sunset picnic.

Start: Yost trailhead
Distance: 4.4-mile out-and-back
Hiking time: About 5 hours
Difficulty: Moderate
Elevation gain: 1,230 feet
Trail surface: Dirt and rock
Hours open: Dawn to dusk
Best season: Early spring to early autumn
Water: None
Toilets: None
Nursing benches: None
Stroller-friendly: No

Potential child hazards: None
Other trail users: None
Dogs: Allowed on leash
Land status: US Forest Service
Nearest town: June Lake
Fees and permits: None
Maps: Inyo National Forest, June Lakes Area map
Trail contact: Inyo National Forest, 351 Pacu Ln., Ste. 200, Bishop, CA 93514; (760) 873-2400; www.fs.usda.gov/inyo
Gear suggestions: Sturdy shoes

FINDING THE TRAILHEAD

From Modesto, take CA 120 east for approximately 110 miles until the road ends at a T-stop. Take a right onto US 395 south for 10.4 miles. Turn right onto CA 158 south for approximately 3 miles until you reach the June Lake Fire Station. Parking will be across the road from the Fire Station at the June Lake trailhead. Parking is somewhat limited, but this trail is lightly trafficked so you should be able to find a spot. GPS: N37 46.98' / W119 4.37'

THE HIKE

Don't confuse this trailhead with the slightly more popular one closer to Silver Lake; the Yost Creek Trail has two trailheads along the June Lake Loop Road, and the *other* end of the U-shaped trail is more frequented. The entire hike makes a beautiful point-to-point day hike, but the roughly 12 miles end to end is likely beyond the interest of most hiking families.

Once you've set off from the eastern trailhead by the Fire Station, the trail quickly jogs up the hill, cuts a quick switchback, and emerges from the trees as it heads southwest along a contour line. Here you'll start to get views of town, and they continue to get better over the next mile. Be on the lookout for bikes coming downhill; this is a local spot and everyone is very courteous, but it also helps if you pull your kids off the trail to make extra room.

After about a half a mile you'll come to a big switchback that gives some of the best views toward town, and even though you're only a quarter of the way to the top, it's worth stopping here to catch your breath and enjoy it. Continue back up the switchback

An early sampler of the views—
you'll feel like you earned them

Continuing along the ridgeline with phenomenal views

Once you gain the ridge, you drift into a flatter, more forested area.

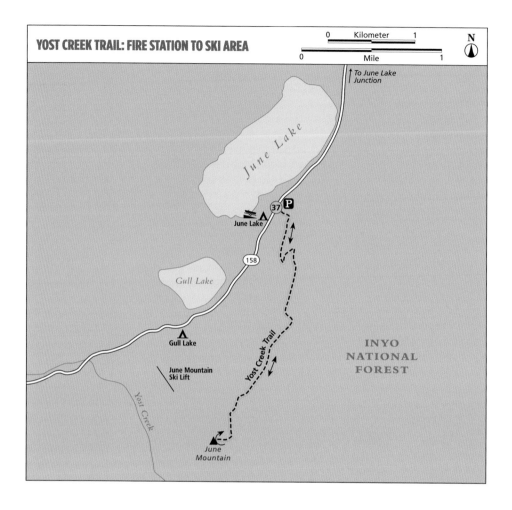

To June Lake
Junction

June Lake

37 P

June Lake

158

Gull Lake

Gull Lake

June Mountain
Ski Lift

Yost Creek Trail

Yost Creek

June
Mountain

INYO
NATIONAL
FOREST

FUN FACTOR: VISIT THE MOUNTAIN HIDEAWAY OF JUNE LAKE

The charming town of June Lake is one of our personal highlights for any trip we take to this region. It retains the small-town charm you expect of a mountain hamlet in the Eastern Sierra, and with all the good day hikes (like this one that practically departs from the city center) nearby, it's easy to fill up a long weekend with plenty of satisfying family fun. After this particular hike we recommend heading over to the beach at June Lake, where there's a protected swimming/wading area for kids at the eastern end with incredible views toward the Sierra Crest. Once the sun dips behind the ridgeline (which happens much earlier than true sunset), head into town to June Lake Brewing for food at one of the food trucks, along with some well-earned adult beverages. Sarah and Justin Walsh are the owners of the brewery, and if you're looking for additional family-friendly recommendations in the June Lake area, you can typically catch one of them on the property and get some expert local advice.

Looking down toward the chalet at the end of the trail

with commanding views of Gull Lake, June Lake, and out farther toward Mono Lake in the valley below, and then after another tenth of a mile you'll turn south again and start to head into a more wooded area. The grade continues up to about a mile, and then it levels off as the trail reaches the top of the ridge. This casual grade continues for about a mile in a beautifully wooded area, and if you have kids who are still in a kid carrier but moderately mobile, this is a good place to set them down and let them have the run of the place. If you time it right, this is also great wildflower viewing with pops of color showing up well in the shaded greenery; expect to see a lot of Indian paintbrush, mule's ears, and sulfur buckwheat.

Continue tracking south/southwest until you come to a very obvious ski run a little over 2 miles from the trailhead. As you pop out of the wooded area, you'll have beautiful views toward Carson Peak, and looking downhill you'll see the June Meadows Chalet. In the winter this serves as the main lodge for the ski hill (it's one of the few we've seen where you take a lift *to* the main lodge), and from its perch at the top of the hill you look directly down into town. We highly recommend bringing a picnic and enjoying a sunset view from near the chalet. For your return, simply retrace your steps and enjoy how much easier it is going back down than coming up.

If you're feeling strong, you can extend this hike all the way to Yost Lake. It adds another 2.5 miles *one way*, but there's not too much elevation change as you've already done most of the hard work.

MILES AND DIRECTIONS

0.0 Begin at Yost trailhead.

1.0 The trail starts to level out.

2.2 Reach the June Mountain Ski Area and return the way you came.

4.4 Arrive back at the trailhead.

ADVANCED HIKES

Late night at camp
above Second Lake

38 BIG PINE LAKES VIA NORTH FORK OF BIG PINE CREEK

This is easily one of the best bang-for-buck overnights in Northern California. The 9.2-mile round-trip hike will require ambition from your kids, but if they're strong enough to hike the 3,000 feet of elevation gain, they (and you!) will be rewarded with sunset views of the inimitable Temple Crag reflected in an emerald, glacier-fed lake. Go in the autumn if you don't mind the cold overnight temps, as the aspen, willows, cottonwoods, and birches all put on an underrated fall color display.

Start: Big Pine Creek trailhead
Distance: 9.2-mile out-and-back
Hiking time: About 7 hours
Difficulty: Strenuous
Elevation gain: 3,000 feet
Trail surface: Dirt and rock
Hours open: Dawn to dusk
Best season: Spring to autumn
Water: Treated water from nearby creeks and lakes
Toilets: At the trailhead
Nursing benches: At North Fork Picnic Area along the trail
Stroller-friendly: No

Potential child hazards: Lots of rock
Other trail users: None
Dogs: Allowed on leash
Land status: US Forest Service
Nearest town: Big Pine
Fees and permits: None
Maps: Inyo National Forest, June Lakes Area map
Trail contact: Inyo National Forest, 351 Pacu Ln., Ste. 200, Bishop, CA 93514; (760) 873-2400; www.fs.usda .gov/inyo
Gear suggestions: Sturdy shoes and trekking poles

FINDING THE TRAILHEAD

From Modesto, take CA 108 east for approximately 30 miles. Merge onto CA 120 east for 107 miles until you turn right just before the town of Bishop onto US 395 south. Continue on 395 for 79 miles where you'll turn right onto Crocker Avenue just before the Shell gas station in Big Pine. Crocker Avenue becomes Glacier Lodge Road after a half-mile. Stay on this road for approximately 9.5 miles until you reach the Big Pine Creek trailhead adjacent to Glacier Lodge. The area is popular for overnight backpacking, but there is a small parking lot right at the trailhead for day-usage. GPS: N37 7.53' / W118 26.25'

THE HIKE

Be sure to park at the overnight use trailhead near the Glacier Lodge; it can be easy to park at the national forest campsite and accidentally add distance to your hike. Start by walking along the Big Pine Creek that runs along the parking lot, then you'll soon cross a footbridge and arrive at the junction for South Fork canyon. The teasing views into the canyon walls may look tempting (and South Fork is a great 5-mile round-trip day hike on its own), but stick to the north and begin switchbacking your way up.

You'll continue hiking along the North Fork of Big Pine Creek on a treeless, exposed hillside. This is one of the most challenging sections of the hike if you undertake this in midsummer, as there is little respite from the alpine sun. We recommend an early start if possible (which is sometimes an impossibility depending on the age of your progeny);

Fall color along the lower
portion of the trail

The water is definitely colder than it looks, but this is still a good idea.

otherwise double-check to make sure everyone has plenty of sun protection. Eventually you will arrive at the top of Second Falls, which is a 100-foot cascade that doubles as the edge of the John Muir Wilderness. This is a nice place to stop for a picnic, as the shade and nearby falls feel considerably cooler than the prior stretch.

Continue along the shaded trail as you steadily ascend toward the next major land-mark, Lon Chaney Sr's cabin. It's now a Forest Service cabin, but its start as a getaway for one of Hollywood's early character actors make for a romantic origin story. Even more noteworthy: The cabin's architect was the prolific Paul Revere Williams, the first Black person granted a fellowship in the American Institute of Architects. He designed homes for Lucille Ball, Frank Sinatra, and other Hollywood luminaries, and he also contributed to public buildings like the Los Angeles County Courthouse.

At about 4 miles you come to another junction that starts the loop toward Second Lake. You've done 2,000 feet of gain and most of the work, so it's worth taking a breather if you want to enjoy the continually improving scenery, like the overlook down to First Lake. Stay to the left (the right would get you there, but it's longer, steeper, and more exposed) and begin the steady ascent to Second Lake. The trees will begin to thin, and you'll have views of the moraines and talus that make up the primary character of the upper parts of the valley.

The main trail continues to the right of Second Lake, but look for use trails that head toward the overlook on the north side of the lake. You'll know it when you see it. Keep an eye out for ideal campsites; please remember to set up shop at least 100 feet from the shoreline, and also in a location that looks previously impacted by other campers. You can also wander the shoreline to find a handful of locations that are suitable for cliff jumping (always scout your landing zone first), although we recommend only doing it when the summer temps can warm you up quickly. Glacially fed lakes can make for a *very* cold day.

This could be your campsite view of Temple Crag.

The Palisade Glacier is not an easy extra-credit hike, but the views are worth it.

FUN FACTOR: HIKE ON A GLACIER

Above Second Lake lies the half-mile-wide Palisade Glacier. It is magnificent, and a unique opportunity in California's backcountry to see something majestic that you cannot view from a road. It is also a serious endeavor and should only be undertaken by families who are confident hiking at altitude and off-trail. To start, leave camp at Second Lake (hopefully with a much lighter pack!) and head toward the predictably titled Third Lake. Cruise up the switchbacks, and eventually you'll come to the beautiful alpine Sam Mack Meadow. From here the trail becomes less maintained as you slowly ascend additional switchbacks before the official trail concludes at 11,700 feet. You'll stare at a giant talus field ahead of you that may be marked by the occasional cairn; these can be useful, but ultimately you should choose the line that gives you and your family the most confidence. Scrambling on boulders can be a lot of fun for the confident hiker, but we would not recommend doing it with a kid carrier. Once you make it to the top, you have a commanding view of the glacier and pool at its base. You may opt to hike the 300 feet down to the glacier for a closer view, or you can take the family selfie from the overlook and carefully begin the return hike back down.

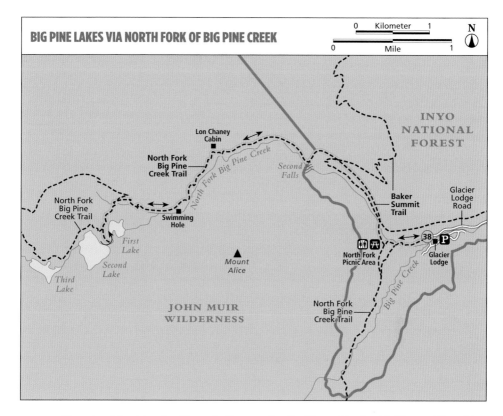

BIG PINE LAKES VIA NORTH FORK OF BIG PINE CREEK

If you've hiked in the Sierra before, you're familiar with the idyllic sparkling, blue alpine lakes that reflect sunshine and granite. Second Lake appears aquamarine thanks to the glacial sediment in the water, and if you catch the afternoon light just right, it will take on an ethereal turquoise hue.

MILES AND DIRECTIONS

0.0 Pass through the gate at the end of Glacier Lodge Road and begin hiking along the access road.

0.2 Reach the actual trail and begin a steep series of switchbacks.

0.8 Continue climbing as the path turns north-northwest.

1.4 Trail junction; stay straight.

2.5 Pass by Cienega Mirth, site of Lon Chaney's old cabin.

4.1 Trail junction; stay left.

4.2 You've reached the high point of your hike.

4.4 Trail junction; stay left and hike into the area between First and Second Lakes.

4.6 Find a nice spot for a picnic or nab a beautiful backcountry campsite. When you're done, retrace your steps.

9.2 Arrive back at the trailhead.

39 GEM LAKE VIA RUSH CREEK

There are many more popular hikes in the Mammoth area, which is precisely why we love this one. It feels like a secret backdoor to an archetypical Sierra high-country lake, complete with granite expanses, plenty of sunshine, and treed shorelines that are perfect for hammocks. Many people do this as a day hike—and it's perfect as such—but we also recommend it for a good starter overnight. The constant source of water makes it easier to keep your pack weight low (although if you have someone in a kid carrier there may be no avoiding it), and if your kids are like ours, they can be easily entertained for hours with a shoreline and some trees to climb.

Start: Rush Creek trailhead
Distance: 6.6-mile out-and-back
Hiking time: About 6 hours
Difficulty: Strenuous
Elevation gain: 2,080 feet
Trail surface: Dirt and rock
Hours open: Dawn to dusk (road to the trailhead closes in the winter)
Best season: Early spring to early autumn
Water: At Silver Lake campground across the road
Toilets: At the parking lot and Silver Lake campground across the road
Nursing benches: None

Stroller-friendly: No
Potential child hazards: None
Other trail users: None
Dogs: Allowed on leash
Land status: US Forest Service
Nearest town: June Lake
Fees and permits: None
Maps: Inyo National Forest, June Lakes Area map
Trail contact: Inyo National Forest, 351 Pacu Ln., Ste. 200, Bishop, CA 93514; (760) 873-2400; www.fs.usda.gov/inyo
Gear suggestions: Sturdy shoes

FINDING THE TRAILHEAD

From Modesto, take CA 120 east for approximately 110 miles until the road ends at a T-stop. Take a right onto US 395 south for 4.4 miles. Turn right onto CA 158 south for approximately 9 miles until you reach Silver Lake campground. Parking will be across the road from the campground at the Rush Creek trailhead. Parking is somewhat limited, but this trail is lightly trafficked so you should be able to find a spot. GPS: N37 46.97' / W119 7.71'

THE HIKE

The first part is the worst part, so if you look up from the trailhead and wonder if the entire hike is going to feel like this, thankfully the answer is no.

Start near the north end of Silver Lake, and the trail tracks south as it steadily heads toward the obvious saddle above you. The trail is steep but well maintained; don't start out of the gates too fast. You'll be well served to take frequent breaks as you get closer to Rush Creek. The creek earns its moniker thanks to the steep grade as it rushes down the hillside, which should give you an idea about how your quads are going to feel as you head the other direction.

As you reach the switchbacks, turn around and soak up the views of Silver Lake. This area claims to be the oldest fishing retreat in the region, and if you have time on your way

The trail heads up toward the saddle on the right, and it's a tough start.

Sunset above a seasonal creek
overlooking the lake

Tents: We love them because toddlers don't know how to get out of them.

FUN FACTOR: TACKLE A MULTINIGHT IN MULTIPLE CAMPSITES

If you're feeling ambitious, this trail is the starting point to one of the most spectacular hikes in the Eastern Sierra. We recommend keeping Gem Lake as the night one destination, and then hiking over to the Thousand Lake area, which is one of the crown jewels of the Ansel Adams Wilderness. This area abuts Yosemite National Park, and has all the same high-country charm as its world-famous neighbor. For our trip we spent one night at Gem Lake, two nights at the same camp on the north shore of Thousand Island, and then a return night at Gem Lake. Thousand Island has spectacular swimming in the summer; even though it's up at 10,000 feet, the days get plenty warm to take advantage of the snowmelt-fed temps. Take one of your sleeping pads and use it like a raft. If your kids are old enough, you can even swim out to one of the eponymous islands. There's also great fishing in the stock lake, so if you don't mind adding a few more ounces to your pack, you can almost guarantee landing a trout or two.

Relaxing in the hammock in our camp overlooking Gem Lake

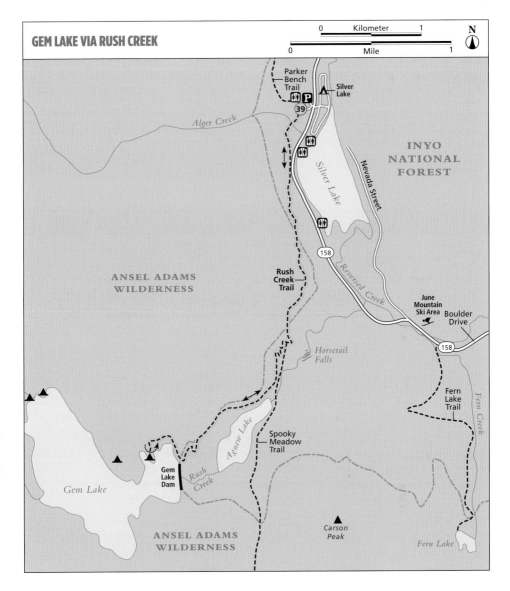

Kilometer

0   1

0   Mile   1

N

Parker
Bench
Trail
39
Silver
Lake

Alger Creek

Silver Lake

Nevada Street

INYO
NATIONAL
FOREST

158

Rush
Creek
Trail

Reversed Creek

ANSEL ADAMS
WILDERNESS

June
Mountain
Ski Area
Boulder
Drive

158

Horsetail
Falls

Fern
Lake
Trail

Fern Creek

Agnew Lake

Spooky
Meadow
Trail

Gem
Lake
Dam

Rush
Creek

Gem Lake

Carson
Peak

ANSEL ADAMS
WILDERNESS

Fern Lake

out of town, find an extra few minutes to stop at the Silver Lake Café on the north side of the lake. There you can see some of the trophy trout mounted on the wall, and even if you're not hungry, it's still worth making space for one of their milkshakes.

As you make your way through the switchbacks, you'll look up and see a set of tramway trail tracks. Lamentably there is not a way to hitch a ride; this was built back in 1915 to service the hydroelectric plant that powered the town. Once you crest the ridgeline, you'll see the Agnew Lake, hemmed in by the Agnew Lake Dam that was built in the same year as the tramway. Take a break here, and once you catch your breath continue southwest along the side of Agnew Lake as you steadily climb in elevation.

Once you past the far end of Agnew Lake, it is not far until you hit Gem Lake, but keep hiking around the northern shoreline because the views and campsites get better as you progress. Our favorite spot is on the northern edge of the lake; it's well protected, well established (please remember to always camp in established campsites), and has moderately easy access down to the shoreline. Incidentally this was also the first place our daughter ever went skinny-dipping, although it was really more so for a backcountry bath than anything else.

After you've had your fill of Gem Lake, take the same route for the return trip.

MILES AND DIRECTIONS

0.0 Begin at the parking area across the road from Silver Lake Campground. Find the trail that leaves from the south side of the lot.

0.3 Beautiful overlook of Silver Lake.

1.3 Cross over a small stream while still ascending.

1.5 Begin a steep series of switchbacks that rapidly climb upwards.

1.9 Trail junction; stay right.

2.0 You'll see Agnew Lake on your left as you traverse along the northwest shore.

2.9 Pass by the Gem Lake Dam.

3.1 You've reached the high point of the hike.

3.3 Identify a nice lunch spot or find a backcountry campsite, depending on your plan. You're now on the north shore of Gem Lake. Once you're done, retrace your steps back to the car.

6.6 Arrive back at the parking area.

40 GLACIER POINT SKI HUT

You can easily visit the iconic Glacier Point in the summer with all of the crowds of people at Yosemite National Park. But we recommend ditching the hordes of visitors, coming in the winter on skis or snowshoes, and treating your older kiddos to a lifelong memory.

Start: Badger Pass Ski Area
Distance: 21.0-mile out-and-back
Hiking time: Overnight (about 16 hours)
Difficulty: Strenuous
Elevation gain: 554 feet
Trail surface: Packed snow
Hours open: Open daily, 24 hours a day
Best season: Winter
Water: At the ski area and ski hut
Toilets: At the ski area and ski hut
Nursing benches: Tables at the ski area and ski hut
Stroller-friendly: No
Potential child hazards: None

Other trail users: Cross-country skiers
Dogs: Not allowed
Land status: National Park Service
Nearest town: Yosemite
Fees and permits: Fee to enter the park, or purchase America the Beautiful annual pass
Maps: Yosemite National Park map
Trail contact: Yosemite National Park, PO Box 577, Yosemite, CA 95389; (209) 372-0200; www.nps .gov/yose
Gear suggestions: Snowshoes or cross-country skis

FINDING THE TRAILHEAD

From San Francisco, take I-580 east for approximately 45 miles. Keep left to continue onto I-205 east for 15 miles following signs for Tracy/Stockton. Merge onto I-5 north briefly and then take exit 461 for CA 120 toward Manteca/Sonora. Stay on CA 120 for approximately 92 miles. Turn right onto Big Oak Flat Road, go for 10 miles, and then turn left onto El Portal Road. El Portal Road turns slightly right and becomes Southside Drive. Stay on Southside Drive for 0.9 mile and then take a right onto Wawona Road for 9.2 miles. Turn left onto Glacier Point Road for 5 miles and park at Badger Pass Ski Area. GPS: N37 43.82' / W119 34.42'

THE HIKE

As the fifth-most-visited park in the country, the iconic Yosemite National Park is a veritable zoo in the summer with thousands of visitors filling the valley on a daily basis. However, the buses and tour groups disappear for the winter, leaving some of California's most sought-after destinations virtually abandoned. Glacier Point is one of them.

Of course, Yosemite's mild winter temperatures will help you. With average lows hovering barely below freezing, it's not a hard sell to tackle a winter adventure. Plus, did we mention there is homemade lasagna at the end?

Perched 3,000 feet above Yosemite Valley, Glacier Point itself is easily one of the most awe-inspiring views in the entire state, let alone the park. From this vantage point, you can clap eyes on Yosemite Falls to the west and Half Dome to the east, with a lot of magnificent alpine scenery packed in between. But, the road to Glacier Point closes in the winter due to heavy snow, so cross-country skis or snowshoes are your only alternatives.

As the mileage indicates, a round-trip adventure to Glacier Point would be quite a large day for even the most experienced of hikers. That's why we recommend breaking

Sunset from an overlook
near the ski hut

Calling it a "hut" is a bit of an understatement.

the trip up by staying at the luxurious Glacier Point Ski Hut (open December–March). In the summer, it pulls double duty as a glorified souvenir shop, but in the winter, the building transforms into a twenty-person backcountry ski lodge with plumbing, a full kitchen, and home-cooked breakfasts and dinners by the on-site chef. Overnight guests can then venture out to other sites (like nearby Taft Point, Panorama Point, and Sentinel Dome) and enjoy the pristine winter views in utter, peaceful solitude.

Of course, you have to get to the hut first.

After securing reservations in advance, begin your journey at the Badger Pass Ski Area, the farthest one can go along Glacier Point Road in the winter before it closes. If you're staying at the hut, grab an overnight wilderness permit here too. Once that's sorted, you'll find the beginning of the road on the north side of the parking lot.

The first half-mile acts as a mellow warmup as the road immediately trends upward, gaining 125 feet of climbing. But at 0.6 mile, you can relax just a bit as the undulating

FUN FACTOR: GLACIER POINT SKI HUT

Twenty-one miles of skiing in one day is a lot for adults and children alike, which is why we highly recommend a night or two at the Glacier Point Ski Hut. The stone-and-log building is a veritable high-country chalet, reminiscent of the huts found in the high alpine of Europe. Inside, visitors will find couches, a woodstove for heat, restrooms, and a twenty-person bunk room (no private rooms). Bedding isn't included, but you can bring your own or rent a Mountain Hardwear sleeping bag at the hut for an additional fee.

route heads back downhill. You'll descend over 400 feet, bottoming out around 3.3 miles. But don't get too excited: What goes down must go up, right?

From here, a steady climb begins and doesn't quit until you've reached mile 7. Between here and there, you'll gain nearly all of the climbing of the day: nearly 1,000 feet.

Sublime views of Half Dome from the trail

GLACIER POINT SKI HUT

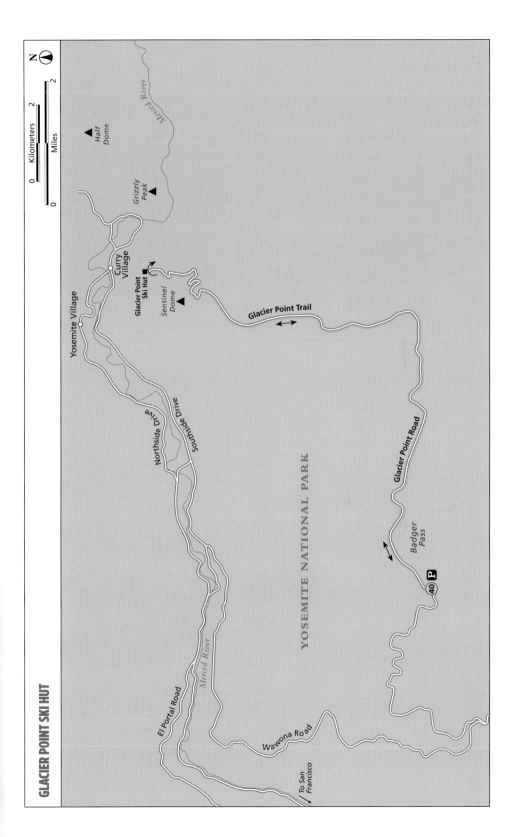

N

0   Kilometers   2

0   Miles   2

Merced River

▲ *Half Dome*

▲ *Grizzly Peak*

Yosemite Village

Curry Village

Glacier Point Ski Hut ■

▲ *Sentinel Dome*

Glacier Point Trail

Northside Drive

Southside Drive

Merced River

YOSEMITE NATIONAL PARK

Glacier Point Road

Badger Pass

P

40

El Portal Road

Wawona Road

To San Francisco

From Glacier Point on a lovely moonlit night

Springtime skiing at its finest

Thankfully, stunning viewpoints along the way make for great respites to break up the ascent. Near mile 6, we recommend stopping at the Clark Range Overlook, a vista that boasts Mount Clark (elevation: 11,506) front and center. To the far left is Cloud's Rest, another beautiful viewpoint in the park. At mile 7, the climbing finally relents and makes way for nearly 2 miles of moderately flat terrain with small bumps interspaced between.

Once you reach mile 9, you know you're close (and can maybe smell the lasagna coming!). From here, you'll descend nearly 600 feet over 1 mile as you lose a large chunk of the elevation you just gained. This time, however, it's a lot more fun since it's downhill. That said, don't let the speed detract from your beautiful surroundings. Even though you're oh-so-close to the hut, we still recommend stopping at Washburn Point at mile 10. Named after two brothers who drove their guests up to this point from Hotel Wawona, Washburn affords skiers an impressive sweeping view of the high alpine. In fact, many people often mistake this overlook for Glacier Point and turn around. Don't do that!

Descend that last half-mile and coast into Glacier Point where you'll find the warm lights and cozy laughter awaiting you from inside the hut. In the blink of an eye, all your hard work and sweat will feel worth it—and your kids will be totally excited for the bunk room.

MILES AND DIRECTIONS

0.0 Start at the Badger Pass Ski Area and find the trailhead on the north side of the parking lot.

0.6 Begin the first descent as trail drops nearly 400 feet over 2.5 miles.

3.3 The ascent begins here and doesn't stop until you've reached mile 7.

6.0 Pass by the Clark Range Overlook on the left side.

7.0 The climbing eases and the rest of the journey is either flat or downhill.

10.0 Pass by Washburn Point and the amazing views of Half Dome.

10.5 You've reached Glacier Point and the ski hut. Retrace your steps back to the parking lot whenever you decide to head home.

21.0 Arrive back at the parking lot.

41 GLEN AULIN

Although the hike is listed as 12 miles round-trip, there's a chance you may only make it half that distance because of the hike's biggest temptation: swimming holes. Although Glen Aulin is a world-class destination in itself, it would still be worth it if you only hiked the 2.6 miles one way to the northwestern edge of Tuolumne Meadows. But for those who do the full route, you'll enjoy some of the most satisfying swimming holes in all of the Sierra High Country, plus a series of waterfalls that make even the hottest days manageable. This hike is beautiful at any time during the summer months, but if you plan on spending time in the water, you're better off going later in the season after water levels drop. The river rages every spring as the snowmelt comes down from the high peaks, and this can be legitimately dangerous for adults, much less their offspring. Come July and August, however, you can find plenty of natural pools with slow currents that are typically safe for water play. Plus the constant supply of water means you can carry a lightweight water filter instead of multiple liters per person.

Start: Tuolumne Meadows Wilderness Center
Distance: 12.0 miles
Hiking time: About 10 hours
Difficulty: Strenuous
Elevation gain: 1,200 feet
Trail surface: Dirt and rock
Hours open: Open daily, 24 hours a day
Best season: Late spring to early autumn
Water: At the trailhead
Toilets: At the trailhead
Nursing benches: None
Stroller-friendly: No
Potential child hazards: Stream crossings and slippery rocks/raging water near waterfalls especially in the spring and early summer

Other trail users: None
Dogs: Not allowed
Land status: National Park Service
Nearest town: Yosemite
Fees and permits: Fee to enter the park, or purchase America the Beautiful annual pass; wilderness permit for overnight trips; reservations for camping at Glen Aulin High Sierra Camp
Maps: Yosemite National Park map
Trail contact: Yosemite National Park, PO Box 577, Yosemite, CA 95389; (209) 372-0200; www.nps.gov/yose
Gear suggestions: Sturdy shoes and trekking poles

FINDING THE TRAILHEAD

From San Francisco, take I-580 east for approximately 45 miles. Keep left to continue onto I-205 east for 15 miles following signs for Tracy/Stockton. Merge onto I-5 north briefly and then take exit 461 for CA 120 toward Manteca/Sonora. Stay on CA 120 for approximately 145 miles. Turn right onto Tuolumne Meadows Lodge Road. Parking is limited at the lodge and wilderness center. GPS: N37 54.56' / W119 25.14'

Views of the Cathedral Range from
the big bend in the Tuolumne River

THE HIKE

You can park at a couple of different spots, which will vary whether you're doing this as a day hike or an overnight. If you're only day hiking, you can generally park anywhere along the dirt road after the Lembert Dome Trailhead as you head toward the stables. Please note that whatever parking you choose, the descriptions below all start from the gate closure on the road to Parsons Lodge.

As you continue on the road you hit several junctions—just continue on the Pacific Crest Trail toward Glen Aulin in a mostly westerly direction and you'll remain on the right path. You may be tempted by side trips to sites like Soda Springs, and if you have extra spring in your step, by all means go ahead and add the mileage, but personally we like to save all the steps for as much river time as possible.

The opening 2.5 miles of the hike are a fairly consistent meander through lodgepole pines, without too much change in elevation or scenery. Just after 2.5 miles you'll reach a sweeping bend in the Tuolumne River, which is also the outreaches of Tuolumne Meadows. Here the river widens and slows, and you have spectacular views to the Cathedral Range to the south. This would be a fitting conclusion for those looking for a shorter hike, and between the Tuolumne and the Dingley Creek forks, there are plenty of places for kids to play.

Left: Looking up toward Tuolumne Falls
Right: Pausing on the Sierra sidewalk before descending down to Glen Aulin

White Cascade, one of our favorite swimming holes in the Sierra

Should you press on, the trail continues mostly adjacent to the Tuolumne River, and the continuous sound of water rushing past granite makes for a wonderful soundtrack. At nearly 4 miles, the trail will begin to head downhill more aggressively, which also coincides with the start of a series of beautiful falls. Enjoy them but keep moving—Tuolumne Falls is just a mile farther! You'll cross a footbridge that moves you to the south side of the river, and at 4.8 miles you'll get your first view of the falls. The view from the trail is impressive, but assuming the water levels are safe, scrambling down to the base of the falls is even better.

FUN FACTOR: GLEN AULIN HIGH SIERRA CAMP

The High Sierra Camps should be on your bucket list's bucket list. You'll see signs for the Glen Aulin High Sierra Camp along this hike, and know that if you're lucky enough to score a reservation, it may ruin backpacking for you just a little bit (but in a good way). The Yosemite National Park Company initially established the Glen Aulin high camp in the 1920s, and today you have a small number of tent cabins to choose from for accommodations. Since you're not carrying a tent and they provide family-style breakfast and dinner, you can hike in with a lightweight day pack and still enjoy the backcountry experience. They'll even include sack lunches if you remember to order one ahead of time! The site itself is near White Cascade, and you'll have lovely sunset views of Mount Conness to end your day.

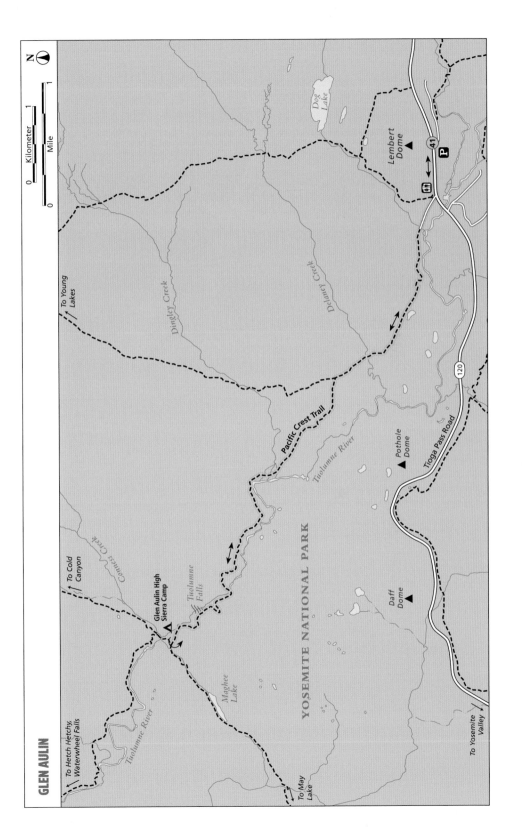

GLEN AULIN

N

0   Kilometer   1

0   Mile   1

Dog Lake

Lembert Dome

41

P

Delaney Creek

Dingley Creek

To Young Lakes

Pacific Crest Trail

Tuolumne River

Pothole Dome

Tioga Pass Road

120

To Cold Canyon

Conness Creek

Glen Aulin High Sierra Camp

Tuolumne Falls

YOSEMITE NATIONAL PARK

Daff Dome

To Hetch Hetchy, Waterwheel Falls

Tuolumne River

Maghee Lake

To Yosemite Valley

To May Lake

Wildlife spotting in Glen Aulin

After marinating in the sunshine for a bit, continue down the trail to the junction with Murphy Creek Trail. Stay north and head toward Glen Aulin, and at 5.2 miles you'll reach White Cascade. This is one of our favorite swimming holes along the entire Tuolumne, as there are pockets deep enough for low-risk cliff jumping (always check the depth first!) and the constant mist from the falls is like living in your own waterpark.

If this is a day hike, consider this your conclusion and start the hike back up and out of the canyon. Remember that the hike out will likely take longer than the hike in, and much of the 1,200 feet of gain is concentrated at the beginning of your return. Take lots of breaks, and if you happened to catch the middle of the afternoon on your way back, consider waiting for a bit more daylight to pass before starting back up.

If you planned for an overnight, you can find designated backpacker campsites just west of Glen Aulin. If you planned multiple nights, this is a great place to set up basecamp and then hike all the way to Waterwheel Falls the next day. This is certainly worth the effort; the undulating pockets in the granite can shoot water several stories into the air, and it's an unusual visual relative to the other cascades you find along the river.

MILES AND DIRECTIONS

0.0   Start on the Pacific Crest Trail at the southwestern corner of the Tuolumne Meadows Wilderness Center.

0.4   Cross Tioga Pass Road.

2.0   Meet up with the Stable Access trail and then cross Delaney Creek.

2.4   Keep left at the fork to stay on the PCT.

3.5   See the first of the waterfalls.

4.7   Cross a footbridge over the Tuolumne River.

5.2   Reach Tuolumne Falls.

5.8   Meet up with the Murphy Creek Trail and take a right to descend to Glen Aulin High Sierra Camp.

6.0   End at Glen Aulin High Sierra Camp and return the way you came.

12.0   Arrive back where you started.

THOUSAND ISLAND LAKE VIA AGNEW MEADOWS

This is alpine paradise. There's a reason why Will has returned to this single location more than any other hike on the planet. The distinctive ridgeline of Banner, the endless sunshine, the massive lake with its own private islands—it matches every bit of Muir's gospel-like hyperbole that you've ever read about the Range of Light. It's also a commitment to get this far into the backcountry. There are no technical sections, so as long as your family has the fitness to walk the required distance, you should approach this with confidence. Although you can certainly do this as an overnight, we recommend 2 nights so you can have a full day to enjoy the Thousand Island Lake area (and a day without a heavy pack!)

Start: Agnew Meadows trailhead
Distance: 15.6-mile out-and-back
Hiking time: About 12 hours
Difficulty: Strenuous
Elevation gain: 4,561 feet
Trail surface: Dirt and rock
Hours open: Dawn to dusk (the road to the trailhead closes in the winter)
Best season: Summer and fall
Water: None
Toilets: At the trailhead
Nursing benches: None
Stroller-friendly: No
Potential child hazards: Stream crossings

Other trail users: None
Dogs: Not allowed
Land status: US Forest Service
Nearest town: Mammoth Lakes
Fees and permits: None
Maps: Inyo National Forest, Ansel Adams Wilderness map
Trail contact: Inyo National Forest, 351 Pacu Ln., Ste. 200, Bishop, CA 93514; (760) 873-2400; www.fs.usda.gov/inyo
Gear suggestions: Sturdy shoes, trekking poles, and lots of sunscreen

FINDING THE TRAILHEAD

From Modesto, take CA 120 east for approximately 110 miles until the road ends at a T-stop. Take a right onto US 395 south for approximately 20 miles. Turn right onto Mammoth Scenic Loop for 6 miles and then turn right onto Minaret Road and go for 4.4 miles. This road will turn into Lookout Point Road/Postpile Road. Stay on Lookout Point Road for 2.7 miles and then turn right onto Agnew Meadows Road. There are multiple parking lots to access the Pacific Crest Trail/Agnew Meadows trailhead. It is also just up the road from the first stop on the seasonal shuttle from Mammoth Mountain ski area. GPS: N37 40.97' / W119 5.13'

THE HIKE

Back in the mid-aughts, this was Will's first hike into the Eastern Sierra, and it completely reconstituted his understanding of the term *wilderness*. After returning many times, Thousand Island was also the destination of our first multinight trip with our daughter, and even though people thought we were out of our minds for taking our 15-month-old on a 5-day backpacking trip, it remains one of our favorite family memories.

Hiking along Thousand Island Lake, just a few minutes from camp

To start, take the shuttle from Mammoth to the Agnew Meadows stop. Walk down the road, past the pack station (you'll know it when you smell it), and on to the lot that's at the actual High Trail trailhead. If your family gets up early you can drive to this trailhead as long as you get through the gate at Minaret Vista, but know that will require an alpine start.

Once you're at the trailhead, you'll bear south/southwest for a moment before turning northwest and linking up with the River Trail about a mile and a half later. This section has a comfortable grade, and it's generally well treed; all the same try to get an early start in the summer as it can get hot in the afternoons. About 2.5 miles from the trailhead, you'll arrive at a junction where you turn left up the Shadow Creek Trail, traverse a bridge over the Middle Fork of the San Joaquin River, and begin a steep section up to Shadow Lake. Take lots of breaks and enjoy the scenery (especially if you're coming from sea level), as each switchback reveals an even better view back down the valley. After ascending 700 vertical feet in a mile, you'll arrive at the peaceful Shadow Lake, which is an ideal spot to stop for a midmorning snack.

The trail remains flat as you wrap around Shadow Lake, and on the far side you'll reach a junction with the famous John Muir Trail where you head north. From here you'll hike up and over a small pass that reveals an incredible view of Garnet Lake; after about 2.8 miles you'll arrive at the mouth of the lake. This is another great spot to rest, and the swimming holes below the bridge are great for kids. We typically stop here for lunch and enjoy the sunshine for a couple hours (there's typically a light breeze that keeps bugs at bay as well) before gearing up for the last leg. It's worth getting out your pillow and stretching out on the smoothed granite slabs that cluster around either side of the bridge, as the sound of the small waterfall and your kids playing in the pool is heavenly. You could

Camp with the ever-present Banner Peak and Ritter Range

Sunrise from the eastern end
of Thousand Island Lake

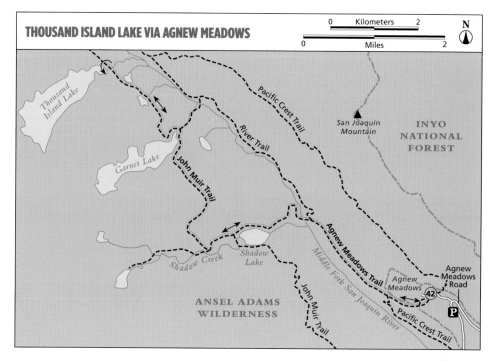

Kilometers
Miles

N

Thousand Island Lake

Pacific Crest Trail

River Trail

San Joaquin Mountain

INYO NATIONAL FOREST

Garnet Lake

John Muir Trail

Agnew Meadows Trail

Middle Fork San Joaquin River

Shadow Creek   Shadow Lake

Agnew Meadows   Agnew Meadows Road

Pacific Crest Trail

ANSEL ADAMS WILDERNESS

John Muir Trail

feasibly stop here and camp along Garnet Lake, although we've found the extra push to Thousand Island is worth it for both the views and the better campsites.

The hardest part is shouldering your pack after a long break, but after the work you've put in so far, the last stretch is fairly manageable. Continue to head north/northwest along the John Muir Trail, where you'll go up one last pass, traverse by Ruby Lake, and then head down toward the mouth of Thousand Island Lake. At this point the view gets better and better with every step; it's worth stopping to take family photos, but if your family has a limit on how many your children are willing to take, save a few for the north side of Thousand Island. There's a small use trail that tracks the north side of the lake, and there are several social trails that wend all over the hillside. Generally the farther you hike from the main junction with the John Muir Trail, the more privacy you'll get. Please respect the request to camp well back from the shoreline, and leave the lakeside spots as day-use only.

If you end up with a layover day and have kids who are looking for a scramble, you can take the 3-mile round-trip hike (as measured from the *far end* of Thousand Island) up to Lake Catherine. This will involve some talus hopping as well as potential snowfield crossings depending upon the time of year, so be prepared for more technical hiking than the previous day. Generally the snowfield is a very low grade by midsummer, and if the snow is soft enough, this can make for a fun way to progress your family's comfort with technical hiking if that's an ambition of yours. The lake itself is classically deep azure and typically dotted with icebergs; looking up toward Ritter and Banner you'll get a beautiful view of the northern route up the glacier to the saddle.

Once you pack up and leave camp, you can opt for the same route on the return, or if you want to trade slightly less mileage for slightly less attractive views, you can take the Pacific Crest Trail to the River Trail for the return route. At the mouth of Thousand

Enjoying a break at the mouth of Garnet Lake

FUN FACTOR: FAMILY SCRAMBLING

If your family is really looking to progress their off-trail skills, you can swap the section of the John Muir Trail between the eastern ends of Garnet and Thousand Island for a gorgeous cross-country scramble below Banner Peak. As you leave the bridge at the end of Garnet Lake, you continue on the MT as previously described, but when you hit the junction after about a mile, continue west alongside Garnet Lake instead of going up and over the pass. Continue to follow this trail until it turns into a social trail at the far end of the lake, then follow the creek that travels mostly west until you arrive below an obvious pass to your north. Choose whichever line looks most comfortable for your family; if you end up doing anything that requires climbing, go back and look for an easier route. Once you crest the saddle, you will see the obvious route down to Thousand Island Lake. Make sure to bear west so you go around the far end of the lake and end up on the north side, as there are more previously established campsites available on that side of the lake.

Hiking up and over the saddle between Garnet Lake and Thousand Island Lake

Island, continue east on the PCT instead of heading back over the pass to Garnet Lake, and after about a mile you'll hit the junction with the River Trail. Although you could technically continue on the PCT, we find the River Trail to be more shaded and generally more pleasant; follow this all the way back to the Agnew Meadows Trailhead.

MILES AND DIRECTIONS

0.0   Agnew Meadows trailhead.

0.5   Stay straight onto Shadow Creek Trail.

1.1   Meet River Trail but stay straight onto Shadow Creek Trail.

2.1   Take a left at the fork on Shadow Creek Trail.

3.8   Stay right to continue on Shadow Creek Trail.

4.5   Bear right (north) onto the John Muir Trail.

7.4   Arrive at the mouth of Garnet Lake, continue straight/north on the John Muir Trail.

9.7   End at Thousand Island Lake's outlet.

19.4   Arrive back at the trailhead.

HIKE INDEX

Bartholomew Memorial Park Trail, 113

Big Pine Lakes via North Fork of Big Pine Creek, 209

Big Trees Loop, 13

Bodie Ghost Town Hike, 118

Boy Scout Tree Trail, 19

Bumpass Hell Trail, 25

Burney Falls Loop Trail, 30

Burst Rock, 123

Cinder Cone Trail, 35

Coastal Trail: Gold Bluffs Beach Section, 40

College Cove Trail, 44

Drury–Chaney Loop Trail, 48

Ebbetts Peak, 128

Elk Head Trail, 53

Fern Canyon Loop Trail, 57

Gem Lake via Rush Creek, 216

Glacier Point Ski Hut, 223

Glen Aulin, 231

Kings Creek Falls, 62

Lady Bird Johnson Grove, 67

Leavitt Meadows to Lane Lake, 134

Lower Yosemite Falls Loop, 139

Manzanita Lake Loop, 72

McGhee Creek Canyon, 145

Methuselah Trail, 150

Minaret Vista Loop, 156

Natural Bridges Trail, 161

North Grove Trail, 166

Patriarch Grove Trail, 172

Rim Trail, 78

Sonoma Overlook Trail, 177

South Tufa Trail, 182

Stoney Creek Swim Area Trail, 84

Stout Memorial Grove Trail, 89

Subway Cave Lava Tube, 95

Thousand Island Lake Via Agnew Meadows, 238

Trail of the Gargoyles: South Rim, 187

Trinity Lakeshore Trail, 100

20 Lakes Basin: Steelhead Lake, 108

Upper Kinney Lake via the Pacific Crest Trail, 192

Wolf House Historic Trail, 198

Yost Creek Trail: Fire Station to Ski Area, 203

ABOUT THE AUTHORS

Heather Balogh Rochfort and **Will Rochfort** are a wife-husband duo specializing in the outdoor industry with a combined 20 years of experience. Their work has been featured in the *Washington Post*, The Weather Channel, REI's *Uncommon Path*, *Backpacker*, *Red Bulletin*, *Outside*, and *Men's Journal*, as well as four previous books. Although Will was born and raised in California, he chased Heather out to Colorado, where they currently reside with their daughter.

THE TEN ESSENTIALS OF HIKING

American Hiking Society

American Hiking Society recommends you pack the "Ten Essentials" every time you head out for a hike. Whether you plan to be gone for a couple of hours or several months, make sure to pack these items. Become familiar with these items and know how to use them. Learn more at **AmericanHiking.org/hiking-resources**

 1. Appropriate Footwear

 6. Safety Items (light, fire, and a whistle)

 2. Navigation

 7. First Aid Kit

 3. Water (and a way to purify it)

 8. Knife or Multi-Tool

 4. Food

 9. Sun Protection

 5. Rain Gear & Dry-Fast Layers

 10. Shelter